To Live Is Christ

TO
LIVE
IS
CHRIST

Nature and Grace in the Religious Life

by R. W. GLEASON, S.J.

SHEED AND WARD·NEW YORK

LIBRARY OF CONGRESS CATALOG CARD NUMBER: 61–7287

NIHIL OBSTAT: JOHN R. READY
            Censor Librorum
            OCTOBER 31, 1960

IMPRIMATUR: ✠ ROBERT F. JOYCE
            Bishop of Burlington
            NOVEMBER 8, 1960

FOURTH PRINTING, JANUARY, 1962

MANUFACTURED IN THE UNITED STATES OF AMERICA

To My Brothers in Christ

Contents

Contents

Introduction

It is impossible fully to understand the religious life, the life of Christian perfection, unless we relate it to the Incarnation of the Son of God. At every juncture in our supernatural life we are confronted with this theandric fact, this figure of God become man. Every line in the spiritual life, every movement of the soul towards God, points directly to the central fact of human history and of all Christian spirituality, Jesus Christ, true God and true Man. This statement does not mean only that Christ is the uniquely perfect model for every virtue. It means more than that. Unless we comprehend the objective centrality of Christ in all Christian thought and endeavor we simply do not understand that the thought and endeavor are *Christian*.

That our ascetical efforts and our thinking should be Christian means that they should be modelled after Christ because, in fact, they are shaped by Him from within. Our following of Christ is a following of Christ *in* Christ, where the very power to follow is given by the one in whose Mystical body we have our life. We are "inserted" into Him, the whole Christ, by the grace of baptism. In Him we quite literally "live and move and have our being." To Him we belong "as members belong to the head." Upon Him we are "grafted," as the branch is grafted on the vine. With Him we share one life, the life that belongs to Him, the life of grace. From Him we receive an interior influence, the vital influence of the head upon the members. All our acts are Christian when they are done in Him, and out of Him no acts are Christian, no matter how much they strive to imitate Him. "You are the members of the body of Christ."

St. Paul has taught, and every Christian has accepted as a reality, this mysterious union with Christ. And God has instructed us that our union with Him is a mysterious, supernatural, quasi-physical reality. But what Christians can forget sometimes is the fact that the Incarnation of the Son of God extends itself in time and space, prolonging itself in the whole of the new humanity He has come to create. From the moment of the Incarnation until the end of time the eternal Father labors to complete this mystical body of Christ. Christ is the "first-born of many sons," and through all history the eternal Father is engaged in bringing this body of Christ to its fullness and the Incarnation of His son to its full complement.

As Christians and specifically as religious, we are really prolongations of the unique figure who was both God and Man, the Incarnate Word of God. The whole character of Christian existence is existence-in-Him. Hence all our activity, as far as possible, should be an activity-in-Him. Our Christian thinking should be a thinking with the Incarnate Word; "Let this mind be in you," as St. Paul says, "which was also in Christ Jesus." Just as our Christian being is a prolongation of the Incarnation, so our thinking and our willing, if it is to be Christian, should be a thinking and willing that is a mystical but real prolongation of the thinking and willing of the Incarnation. This truth will be repeated many times, without apology, in the pages which follow, since it is an insight which has been too much neglected, in view of its central significance.

To Live Is Christ

"That They May Be One"

1 "That They May Be One"

It is regrettable but true that religious are often unaware of the real nature of their life in common. One of the fundamental reasons for this deficiency is a certain failure in theological insight and an ignorance of the very meaning of the virtue of charity, the heart of common life. It is easy for religious to enthrone charity as the queen of the virtues, to proclaim it the nourishing mother of all others, and at the same time to live without understanding what it actually is and does. They esteem it as one of many virtues to be cultivated, along with obedience, recollection, modesty, and various others, but they never come to realize that the precise purpose of the religious life is growth in this one central virtue which has, for its double object, love of God and love of neighbor.

We cannot look on God with charity if we do not gaze upon our neighbor with the same eyes of love, for he who loves God also loves his neighbor (1 John 4:21). It is equally impossible to love our neighbor truly without truly loving God, for if we love one another God abides in us and His

5

love is perfected in us (1 John 4:12), and we know that we love the children of God when we love God (1 John 4:2).

This virtue is supreme in Christianity, its theoretic primacy recognized long before in the Old Law. Much of that law, however, with its many precepts, spoke out only on matters of minor importance. This high love for God and neighbor is in direct response to a divine mandate and not to man-made laws. Judaism heard in this mandate a revelation of the inner nature of God Himself, His moral will enunciating His inner character. This was God calling for a tender heart and not merely for external sacrifices (Osee 6:6). In the Old Testament indeed the law of love of God and the neighbor was venerated as the most comprehensive statement of the will of God. Every school of rabbinical theology labored to produce commentaries on this unique principle. In the New Testament John and Paul summarize revelation in the idea of love. For both of them this love is essentially a ray illuminating for us God's own nature. Man is required by the moral law to love because he is required to fashion his life on the model of One who is Himself love. Thus Christ has urged us to imitate the eternal Father by imitating His love for His creatures.

From the beginning, Our Lord made it clear that this central theme of love would differentiate His teaching from that of the other contemporary masters of Israel. The Christian is called, for instance, to be perfect even as the heavenly Father is perfect. In their original context these words signify imitation of the divine love and mercy. This is clearly what Christ intended, for His own life reveals sympathy, tenderness, a heart full of generosity and eagerness to serve, and this can only mean that His love is the instant imitation and revelation of the Father's love for men.[1]

The heart of the Johannine synthesis of the new morality is not reached until the evangelist expounds the notion of agape, or love. This love for our neighbor is the vital center of his teaching. Its high theological importance is clear when we observe that agape looks first of all to God Himself and then to Christ, the bearer and revealer of God's love to and for us. It is an essentially supernatural life which we are commanded to nourish in imitation of the very nature of God. For in John, agape is no longer used merely to signify one or other divine attribute but indicates that which John considers the divine essence itself. The message delivered to us Christians is therefore the same as that spoken to Israel under the former covenant: imitate the Lord, for your moral perfection is to be based upon an imitation of His. "Beloved, if God has shown such love to us, we too must love one another. No man has ever seen God; but if we love one another, then we have God dwelling in us, and the love of God has reached its full growth in our lives" (1 John 4:11, 12).

It is imperative therefore that all our justice before God should be experienced as a received justice and as an impulse to the giving of that which we have received—charity itself. In biblical thought our love is always a replica of the divine essence, and it is only in this light that we can fully comprehend Christian charity. For its wellspring is within the Trinity itself.[2]

As Christians we know that every period of history has been scarred by some deformation of religious attitudes, especially through invasions of formalism, ritualism and casuistry. When Christ spoke to Israel it was in an effort to bring her back to her primitive, burning zeal for fulfillment of the will of God. This is the meaning, for example, of the parable of the Good Samaritan, which so shocked the Israelite consciousness. The Fathers of the Church always saw Christ Himself as the Samaritan, for this attractive allegoric figure embodies Our Lord's fundamental religious message. Christianity is a religion of the service of one's brother.

Our Lord Himself was ever a man of infinite mercy. Indeed, the very credentials of His messianic mission, as He enumerates them for the Baptist, are works of mercy: the blind see, the lame walk, the lepers are cleansed and the deaf hear. And all this is more than a reference to the servant of Yahweh. It is a demonstration through action of the great love which Jesus had for souls. Before attempting to instruct others in charity Jesus lived it Himself in a practical way and proved emphatically that he was replacing a religious conception in which man moves directly from himself to God with a broader vision, in which man's religious life centers upon the neighbor as well as upon God. To the Christ all individuals retain their individuality, and He refuses to distinguish Jew from Gentile or Samaritan from Jew.

This is especially evident in the tremendous scene of the Last Judgment where Christ is revealed as the Lord of history, and at the same time as He who opens the meaning of history to us. The moment of history is the moment which allows us to work by charity for the Lord. Though He is no longer visibly among us, ours is yet the happiness of serving Him in the persons of other Christians. It is these small, every-day kindnesses which, in this final age of the Church, count with Christ. Indeed, time itself is given to us that we may grow in charity. Each encounter with a fellow man is somehow an encounter with the living Christ. Although the term "identification" may be too strong to describe the relationship between Christ and the Christian, yet there is some kind of mystical substitution intended, for Christ Himself has said: "When you did it to one of the least of my brethren here, you did it to me" (Mt. 25:40). We have to go beyond any merely juridical imputation of identity here. There is something profoundly real, although hidden in the darkness of mystery and supernatural, in Christ's oneness with the Christian.

Our everlasting destiny, then, is to be judged by the charity towards God and man which we have developed and caused to grow in us during these last times. The vivifying substitution of Christ for the Christian gives a supernatural character to all our human relationships and brings to a new focus the Jewish teaching on our obligation to love both God and man. Neighborly charity is the whole of Christian perfection because it is a radical imitation of God, and those who do works of charity will be called children of the most high God. Fundamental to all this is the idea that our neighbor is a mystery, a sign of God both revealing and concealing the reality which He represents. St. John remarks bluntly that anyone who says he loves God and yet hates his brother, the same is a liar. For he who loves not his brother whom he sees cannot love God whom he has not seen. Nor does charity merely stop short at not wounding the neighbor. St. Paul tells us that charity goes far beyond this, for it actually makes us slaves one to the other. In this sense too it is apostolic testimony to the divinity of the Church and to the presence of Christ in those who exercise it. For Christ prayed in His high-priestly prayer that we might all be one as He is one with the Father, and that the

Father's love for Him might be in us. To perceive this unity and this divine love is to receive some faint indication of the love wherewith God loves His eternal Son, and in this love mankind as well.[3]

Charity thus enables us to have a share in the divine fellowship which exists in the Trinity itself, and from this deep center we move out to love all of God's creatures. Charity, according to St. Thomas, is friendship, and therefore we love the neighbor for God. At the same time the destination of our love is each concrete individual whom we encounter; otherwise we could not call charity friendship. To all we wish that same divine blessedness which is our own final destiny. Either I love God, myself and all men or I love no one. I must love in the double unity of this virtue. An act of the love of God is distinct from an act of the love of neighbor, but it is impossible for me to exclude a single one of mankind from my charity without excluding God and all others. The neighbor always represents to me, almost as a sacramental symbol, the reality of God Himself with whom he is mystically united.

We discover the transcendent God in this life through the vision of faith, particularly when we look upon the poor and the dispossessed. Brotherly love for the members of Christ's Mystical Body is the living sign of my love for God Himself. Charity is in this sense an epiphany of that future blessedness in heaven when God Himself will be the object of our common joy. Hence my vocation as a Christian is an immediate call, not to isolation, but to a community binding me to all other men. It is at baptism itself that this deeply personal summons is issued to each of us—to enter into fellowship with all the other members of the Mystical Body. Consequently, our conception of human life must be communal. Our deepest contacts with one another can be made only through God, and it is only when we enter into that common movement which bears the neighbor and ourselves mysteriously towards our ultimate goal that we can realize ourselves fully and establish genuine union with one another. It is only love which enables us to co-operate with the central theme of the other individual personality.

Charity gives to all human activity that note of authentic humanity which is the gift of the spiritually free. The Christian is expected to mediate God's love to others in much the same way that Christ mediated to mankind the love of the eternal Father. By initiating his neighbor into God, the Christian lives out the charity of Christ, and through contact with the neighbor he also fulfills himself. Bearing witness to the love of the Father for the Son and of the Son for the Father, our love for the neighbor appears as a temporal manifestation of the eternal Trinitarian relationship. It is in the Son that the Father enables us to contemplate His love for us, and it is the Holy Spirit which enables us to perceive this love for Christ. Christ is the source of our reciprocal love, and at the same time our love is patterned upon this source. In virtue of the love which they give to one another Christians have a role not unlike that of the mystery of generation in the Godhead itself, since in charity they are to awaken in their neighbor's heart new love for God Himself. As the Three Persons of the Blessed Trinity communicate with one another in eternal joyfulness, so also Christian charity suggests to us that our hearts be opened and that we be in communication with all our brethren. Charity is thus the living bond which unites God to the Christian and his fellow men.

The religious above all should realize this truth, that it is impossible for him to fulfill his vocation in spiritual isolation, that when Christ calls upon us to imitate the nature of God by loving, He is calling upon us to fulfill our own nature as He has made it. Unless we transcend ourselves and our own selfishness by making a gift of ourselves to the community, it is impossible to fulfill our created nature, which, as we have seen, derives its relational character from the Trinity itself.

It is impossible also for us to come to adulthood without personal relationships. Perhaps this is one of the reasons why many religious seem never to reach the point of spiritual maturity in which childhood resentments and affective disorders are abandoned and personal adulthood is achieved through balanced altruistic love for others. The religious who is closed, uncommunicative or impersonal in his relationships with others cannot grow in sanctity. God has made men with their own proper autonomy and subjectivity, and the religious must address himself successfully to this, setting up mature relationships of affection and love, if he is to grow to the adulthood of his moral personality. There is nothing in well-ordered human affection which Christ suppresses or truncates; rather He elevates, orders and enriches all that is good in family friendship, in love for the community, in love for inanimate nature itself. Charity, and here we mean also fraternal charity, should be a form ordering all our lesser virtues to God, our final end.[4]

The concept of fraternal charity which would by-pass humanity in order to reach God is an implicit denial of the Incarnation of the Son of God. In loving man aright one also loves God, who communicates His grace and supernatural gifts to mankind. All our virtues become Christian and incarnational in so far as they reflect the character of Christ Himself. And we are fully aware from the Gospels what a central role fraternal charity occupies in the life of Christ. It is this virtue which enables the religious to open the deepest strata of his soul and to meet others in a genuine communion in which both enter into the common stream of grace which moves them towards the Eternal City.

As long as religious are not imbued with a theological understanding of charity they cannot, as we remarked at the outset, grasp the significance of a life lived in common. Hence their formation should have a solidly dogmatic dimension. Too often their instruction produces attitudes of observance but only the most feeble grasp of the meaning of religious virtues and their relative importance and hierarchical order. As a result young people can be misled into thinking supremely significant those religious customs and rules which are at times simply an effective means of maintaining external discipline. Instead, it is the theological virtues which must always be stressed in the training of religious, and particularly the virtues of faith and charity.

Again, the religious must be brought to realize that since every growth in union with God is at the same time an increase of apostolic effectiveness, he or she should not make the lamentable error of creating a wall of separation between personal values and the sacrifices of common life. What fulfills the human personality most completely is that which brings it most closely in union with all other members of the Mystical Body: charity. The intensification of the individual values of each personality is brought to its completion by the spirit of sacrifice which common life fosters through union and charity.

St. Augustine understood this well. For him common life

was essentially the external expression of that fraternal charity which should animate religious living in common. Consequently, he sets charity at the very center of common life, as its very reason for existence. Before him St. Basil had strongly accented the importance of charity in the religious life. He had, in fact, a rather low opinion of those ascetics who lived apart from community life precisely because he could not understand how they were able to exercise fraternal charity. As Christians, he maintained, we are called to salvation as a body, and we have to work and to bear one another's burdens within the unity of the Mystical Body: if one wastes one's talents, or hides them from the common life, one cannot easily fulfill all the precepts of the Gospel. The purpose of monastic life is evangelical perfection itself, that is to say, a higher form of union with God and His Mystical Body. Since men need one another in daily life, they will find in community living mortification for their lower instincts and the opportunity to express love for the neighbor.

St. Thomas developed this idea still further, pointing out that religious observances are not to be judged more perfect simply because they are more severe. Rather they are to be judged more perfect according as they lead more closely to a common life, namely, charity.

St. Augustine visualized the ideal Christian community as something similar to that primitive community at Jerusalem established by the apostles, which had for its purpose the union of hearts and minds in charity. For him, charity takes precedence over everything else, and since all the problems of common life are to be related to charity, only in the light of this precept will they fall into their natural and proportionate place. It is charity which explains the prescriptions of the rule that suffice to unite hearts living in common. The exercise of obedience, of authority, and of all the religious virtues he sees as centered in and dominated by the need to find expression for charity. Community life, to him, is a form of "organized love."

In this Augustine was simply echoing an even more ancient tradition dependent upon revelation itself. We know, for example, that at the time of Christ there already existed a sect called the Essenes who lived in a community which held prayers in common, ate at a common table, and maintained property in common. The Dead Sea Scrolls and the discoveries of the Judean desert have also shown the existence of a monastery which dates from several centuries before Christ. A great building planned for community life, with its own cemetery, its own common room and writing room, has been brought to light at Kumran, and a rule for a sort of religious community implying a genuine monastic life has also emerged. The existence of such a group of men throws light on St. John the Baptist, who baptized only a few miles from Kumran and who had lived for a long time in the desert with his disciples. Such a common life, therefore, was not new in the Old Testament.

Moreover, from the very beginning of revelation we notice that God seeks to form Israel as a holy community. Having before Himself not merely a group of individuals but a theocratic community, He chooses Israel as a people and sets her apart according to a law of solidarity. Indeed this community sense of ancient Israel is almost too well known to need further comment. Even the questions of personal immortality and retribution were not clearly formulated for centuries of Jewish history because of this extraordinarily profound sense of solidarity in the community. On the one hand, kings bring about disasters which afflict the entire people; on the other, the marks of favor recorded by Yahweh are always given to the community itself.

The New Testament insists equally upon this fraternal solidarity. Christ introduces us to the new solidarity of the Mystical Body. As Adam had worked to our damnation, so Christ, as head of the new race, has worked to our redemption. The Church is the new Israel, and she is the ark of salvation. She has the task of building up her members towards a common sanctity, and it is within her, not outside her fold, that salvation is obtained.

Christ Himself had formed a community of charity with His disciples (in which, as we have seen, He was foreshadowed by John the Baptist—it seems, in fact, that several communities of a reforming character existed in Palestinian Judaism at the time of Christ). In the first days of the Church, as we learn from the Acts, the apostles had formed that primitive community at Jerusalem which Augustine regarded as the ideal model of community life. This Christian community made converts and grew to the number of 120 members who prayed together and prepared to receive the Holy Spirit under the guidance of Mary. Later there followed astonishing numbers of conversions, and the Acts hint that some form of common life continued in Jerusalem during the first few years after the death of Our Lord. Its details are not known to us, but there does seem to have been some sharing of property in the apostolic church of Jerusalem.

Common life can provide an exceptional context for the flowering of fraternal charity, and the New Testament often underscores this value. A constant viewpoint in St. Paul's spirituality is that of the mystery of Christ prolonged in His Church and forming a spiritual solidarity with all Christians whose head He is. Consequently all Christians are linked together and, as Paul put it, form one person in Jesus Christ. St. Paul does not hesitate to draw the conclusion that since we are all one body in Christ we should therefore love one another. For the members of a body provide one another with mutual assistance. The whole theological basis for fraternal charity is provided by this mystical "identification" of the Christian with Christ which we touched upon above. In loving men we love God, and in loving men with divine charity we practice a theological virtue. The substitution of a neighbor for Christ is therefore a fundamental theme in both St. John and St. Paul. The love which we have for our brothers is our way of imitating God's love for us. We are urged to love our brothers because God dwells within them and loves them. Our vocation as children of God is to share in the love which Christ has for the Father and for mankind. By fraternal charity we enter into that union with Christ which is an imitation of his union with the Father. It is evident from the whole Gospel of St. John, and even more particularly from his epistles, that we imitate the life of God by acting out our love for the brother. We are thus a visible sign of the Church among men. The presence of Christ is borne witness to by the Church and the Christian community through this love which men have for one another. Christ present in each of us loves all.

The great originality of Christian love consists in the fact that when properly understood it is seen to be a theological virtue, which unites us with our last end. We love our neighbor not because of any natural created goodness in him, not even the supernatural created gift of sanctifying grace, but because in some unknown way he represents Christ. In a mysterious fashion Christ is present to him, and in loving him we love the Christ. We begin our eternal life, which is a life of love here on earth, by loving our neighbor for a motive that refers to God Himself. For true charity is love which finds its source in God. So it is that the whole Church will always have at its core a community of soul between the members of the Mystical Body based upon an acceptation of faith in the words of Christ. The community of the Church descends to us from God, its author and spouse, and the life of this Church is marked by charity.

In view of this understanding of theological charity the mistake of those devout persons who imagine that a chasm divides the apostolate from the virtues of the interior life becomes clear. They need to understand that everything which unites them more fully to God in the interior life is of service to the apostolate at the same time. Charity, as we have said, is a single virtue with one twofold object, God and man. All the virtues that are required for the apostolate or for the external blossoming of common life are fostered in the interior life itself. In the measure in which one becomes a more perfect cell in the Mystical Body, one increases in grace, and in the measure in which one enters more fully into a life of union with Christ as head of the Mystical Body, one advances in an authentic fraternal charity, itself the basis for an authentic common life. It is the identical principle of charity which builds up the social body of a religious community and the personal sanctification of the individual in this community. Hence common life implies no destruction of individual personal values, no submersion of the individual in an impersonal collectivism. This latter notion could only be based upon a false idea of personality itself.

There are, in fact, a number of mistaken conclusions falsely drawn from the philosophic definition of a person. It is true that the notion of person implies self-unity, self-autonomy and incommunicability. However, this does not mean that a person is cut off from relatedness to others. Quite to the contrary, as we have seen, the human person is a miniature of the relational life that is lived among the persons in the Trinity and the ultimate model of community life is precisely this Trinitarian life as it is lived by Father, Son and Holy Spirit.

Today, man is fully aware of social values and the values which attach to communities. And humanity is constantly looking for social forms of existence in which the individual personality may contribute to the common good. In all classes of men who have awakened to the Church's call for union, peace and social justice, there is an ardent desire for those values which are found so easily in a community life of one sort or another. Individualism is no longer the fashion in piety or religious life as it was in the nineteenth century. Hence young religious should understand that they do not walk alone along the way of their personal spiritual fulfillment. Although some pious books have insisted overmuch upon the need for "going it alone" in the spiritual life, this is an individualism savoring not of Catholicism but of Protestantism. The truly Catholic spirit, so appreciative of the genuinely *Catholic* aspects of the Church and the Mystical Body, sees no contradictory tendencies in a community life which is at the same time richly interior.

The Mystical Body of Christ, which is the Church, should be realized in each member according to his vocation. Hence the individual religious should be taught from the beginning that the purpose of the common life is charity. The mutual interdependence characteristic of this life is not simply a means to greater order or to proper religious observance, but a mode of development in depth in the life which is proper to the Mystical Body. If charity is slighted, what we have is no longer a common life but only a material juxtaposition of individuals seeking to collaborate in the same social tasks. This may be in itself an excellent thing, but it is not the traditional form of the common life maintained in the Church. All Christianity is in a sense a true common life because it is a mutual co-existence. Our vocation, as we have seen, is to enter the Church and be saved in it, not as isolated individuals but as members of a body enjoying a common life which flows to us from Christ, its head. The shared life of a religious community is a visible manifestation of this common life of the Church and should be thought of as witnessing to the mystery of the Church herself, the bride of Christ, whose holiness depends in part on the deeper insertion of the individual into herself.

If from the beginning the individual religious is not inoculated with this point of view in regard to common life, very peculiar deformations are likely to appear, veiling themselves under the name of common life. For example, not infrequently the life which was ordained to foster charity is actually turned by certain religious into a means of fostering selfishness. Those who enter in order to donate themselves, their gifts and their energies, to the community appear after a number of years in religious life to have acquired the selfishness, the pettiness of hardened bachelors and spinsters. They insist that every detail of life must be organized to their own convenience, and little by little they eliminate from common life as many of its more trying aspects as possible. With the security of the community enfolding them and without the ties and concerns of family and business life, they become adept at avoiding responsibility and work of all sorts, while claiming for themselves a constantly increasing comfort within the bounds of common life.

Another unfortunate deformation is the result of an excessive submersion of the individual in common life with a consequent abandonment of all individual responsibility. There are certain priests, brothers and nuns who constantly assert that responsibility for the success or failure of common enterprises belongs not to them but to the superior. They prefer to float along on the stream of their order's accepted traditions without contributing anything personal or without vitally absorbing or understanding these traditions. Whatever is done in the particular community in which they live, whether or not it be in accordance with the genuine spirit of their institute, is to their liking. They shy away from the slightest responsibility or decision, gradually losing the characteristics of sharply defined personalities.

Still others feel that they are called to an interior life with God of such depth and intimacy that they must shut themselves off from any genuine, vital, sympathetic communication with the rest of the community. This of course is an extreme error, since even in the most contemplative community the members are called upon to exercise openness, devotedness, self-immolation and kindness towards one another.

At times it is the community itself, as a whole, which

wanders from the ideals of common life. Thus when a particular religious community is overworked a certain selfishness in the individual members can gradually emerge and effectively prevent the pooling of activities towards a common end. Each one works, but only as a rather isolated individual. The result is a mere superficial semblance of common activity. When this happens the flame of charity flickers and dies in the chilling breeze of excessive individualism. Common life then, instead of being a support to religious, becomes merely a burden, each one seeking his own interests under the guise of a cool cordiality which one would never dare to penetrate with an honest appeal for help. It is a fact that in many religious communities people will confess that they know almost nothing about the personal lives of those with whom they live—the sorrows, the joys, the interests or the work of their fellow religious. Obviously in such cases the stream of charity which should flow within the individual community has failed.

The search for independence so characteristic of religious today can serve to propagate this pseudo-common life in which individuals seek only their own interest. The tremendous activity characteristic of today's religious groups is a threat to common life because it nourishes these tendencies to distraction and to individualism. On the other hand, as we indicated above, a collectivism in which the individual personality becomes completely colorless is also destructive of fruitful common life. That is why it would be helpful if instructions to religious families were to inculcate a dogmatic understanding of common life, instead of overemphasizing the moral aspects; or if, besides explaining the personal, individual aspects of piety, they were also to show clearly how common life is a function of charity. It seems almost unthinkable that a group of religious should share the same household, the same spiritual traditions, and yet find fraternal charity lacking in daily intercourse. It is distressing to find the members of a community refusing to give to one another the support, encouragement and understanding that are part of the religious life. This is frequently due to a simple lack of perception on the part of superior and subject alike. The primacy of charity must be constantly stressed; otherwise we fall back into our natural selfish individualism wherein we magnify small differences of opinion and where vanity, jealousy and, at times, something closely resembling hatred are apt to appear.

It is true that common life promotes various virtues simply because of the conditions by which different temperaments, tastes and ages are brought into unity, and natural motives such as arise from the common task and the sharing of burdens can be put to use in the religious life; but these motives cannot take the place of that which is primary, charity, without destroying or naturalizing the notion of the common life. That Christian community life is an imitation of the divine Trinitarian life of charity must always be kept in mind if we do not wish to find ourselves with mere caricature at the end.

Community life is an apprenticeship for mortification and a successful apostolate. It is also a condition for the apostolate, as St. Ignatius stressed repeatedly. He himself effected a beneficial development of common life by putting less emphasis on the observance of exterior discipline and more on the inner spirit of charity which should unite, under diverse circumstances, the members of his order.

There are dangers implicit in all social organization, and superiors must exercise certain precautions if the harmony of the community is to be preserved. First they should see to it that the personalities entering religious life are suitable for leading a life in community.

We all know the levelling effect of group activity and group life. It is possible that the least common denominator will be accepted as the norm if one is not careful. Sociologists have pointed out that if the level of intelligence in a certain group is varied, it will normally be the lower or medium intelligence which will exert the most influence. We must be aware of these factors, therefore, before deciding who may be allowed to embark upon the common life.

The action of the group with regard to the individual members must not be overlooked when we consider common life. Each one who enters religious life becomes part of a family with great traditions and should be allowed to feel fully accepted and loved by the family and esteemed as a useful member of the community. Hence it would be psychologically and sociologically wrong to allow peculiar personalities to enter into common life, since they might later be pushed aside or ignored, with disastrous results to themselves and to the community. Moreover there must be active charity shown to those who are in the religious state, so that they feel the inner peace which "belonging" gives.[5] Only under such conditions can certain people be led gradually to abandon the defensive, suspicious attitudes which cause so much unhappiness. There would be much less envy, much less individualism, boasting, and striving to obtain the best in religious communities if the individual religious felt that he or she was really accepted and loved.

Generous aspirations and noble talents can only flourish in a healthy atmosphere of mutual security and trust which is real and not merely verbal. The individual must always be made to feel that he is useful and that his talents are recognized. Hence one should not try to force all members of the community into the same mold or to neutralize God-given individuality and gifts. There have been religious superiors who confessed that they were able to understand only one sort of person. Anyone falling outside the area of this one type was automatically excluded from understanding and security and made to feel unwanted. Obviously this is entirely wrong, for if the approval and affection to which every member of the community is entitled are withdrawn, or if they are merely verbal, the talents God has sent to the institute will not develop, and undesirable attitudes will appear. Bitterness, for instance, will often be fostered by this feeling of lack of support. The individual's personality grows only through a genuine gift of himself to common effort, as he learns to co-ordinate personal activity with group activity.

Normally speaking, a healthy personality is the best basis for a healthy spirituality, and a healthy personality requires relatedness in giving, in generosity and self-donation. The superior therefore must always see to it that he or she creates an atmosphere in which initiative and authority are organically united and in which each member is encouraged, not to passivity, but to the making of a legitimate personal contribution. There is nothing wrong in asking individuals to give their opinions as to the difficulties and problems in common life. Those who are closer to given situations often have an insight which escapes superiors.

Hence minorities in the community should be allowed free exposition of their viewpoint. This will allow them to accept later decisions with equanimity.

Common life too requires certain adaptations in our modern world. For example, defects or difficulties in the observance of the law should not be dealt with exclusively at the level of authority and from above. Rather, the entire group should be invited to express their opinions objectively concerning those difficulties of organization, time, order, and so on, which make the observance of the rule more difficult. If the superior behaves as though the members of the community have nothing to contribute, as though its affairs are his exclusive prerogative which must meet no opposition, then the subjects will fall into undesirable passivity. If a certain amount of group discussion, controlled by the superior yet frank and open, is not permitted, it will sometimes happen that the subjects, and even the council, will slavishly agree to everything that is suggested by the superior and expect all the initiative to come from him simply because they have learned that it is useless to make suggestions.

It is, of course, indispensable that the superior correct his subjects according to the institute. Nevertheless, the pressure for correction exerted by the group itself after thorough and open discussion of the difficulty is often much more beneficial. When the problem is formulated on this objective level resentment is not created within the community, and all the aspects of the difficulty can be brought out more clearly when more than one opinion is heard.

There can be in a community, as we have observed, a well-organized semblance of friendliness which is actually rather mechanical—a surface affair involving no genuine contact of personalities. In certain such communities superiors even avoid giving orders for fear that they will be met with resentment or disobedience. Or, again, subjects refuse to point out to superiors objective difficulties in any task assigned to them, either because they do not want responsibility or because they are indifferent to the concerns of a community which has shown itself to be not a body of charity but a more or less efficient team working for objective goals.

Psychologically this is undesirable, since behind the mask of an artificial politeness feelings of frustration and even deep bitterness can be engendered in the subject denied the possibility of objectively and openly explaining the difficulties that he or she is experiencing. Repressed violences are likely to break out in strange little gusts of passion otherwise unrelated to the real problem. The community is supposed to be a social body, and it should have the healthy signs of any sound group or organization. Frankness and sincerity are therefore the essence of any community life. Monks, nuns and brothers should be trained to express their convictions firmly on the problems that relate to the community life and to listen objectively and interestedly to the opinions of others. This frank exchange of views frequently does more for the situation than any command from on high.

It would help a great deal—to return to a suggestion indicated earlier—if persons allowed to enter religious life were selected with extraordinary care.[6] It is a well-known fact that certain withdrawn types of personality, unable to make a healthy adjustment in the outside world, gravitate towards the religious life. Although their adjustment to that form of life may seem to be successful, in reality they con-

tribute little to the good of the community or to their own
personal development. Shunning responsibility, they gradually return to a state of childlike dependence upon the
superior and the rule.

Such withdrawn, aloof personalities should be forbidden
entrance. For they are normally incapable of those free and
open relationships which create an agape, or community
of love. Their contact with other people is weak, lacking
the warmth which allows them to contribute to the general
social life. Communities accepting such persons will later
find that their refusal to do anything useful, their shrinking
from contact, conflict, or decision, their frequently scrupu-
lous tendencies can end in a state of paralyzed inactivity.

The personality best suited for common life is one which
could adjust well in the world. For this reason it has been
wisely urged that religious, especially those whose common
life is very closely organized, make use of psychological
examinations before admitting subjects. A religious community should be "open" to the members, to the group, to
the world. Each community has some apostolate of service
and of prayer, and the personalities engaged in this should
be capable of normal, well-balanced relationships with
other human beings.

The community should also, in view of the levelling factor
we have described, make every effort to determine for itself what standard of intelligence and culture is called for
by its apostolate and then adhere to this norm in accepting
candidates. In some communities of women in which the
tone has been set by those who have come from a narrow
socio-cultural background and are at the same time of
limited intelligence, recreations center on the most trivial
topics and are maintained at a level of unintellectual piety

which would inevitably repel normal, well-educated women. This is unfortunate, since recreation ought also to be an educative process. From time to time the superior should enter the discussion to point it up to a more positive and intellectual level. This can be done without interfering with freedom or producing constraint.

In certain communities of religious men the downward pull of those with few intellectual interests may impose an almost steady diet of conversation about sports. While this may be absorbing for a while, the major interest of this group is presumably not athletic prowess. Religious should be encouraged to discuss matters on the same informed level as any other professional group. Lawyers, doctors, and educators often discuss the problems of their profession in recreation.

In other words, one must keep in mind that common life requires, as Pope Pius XII has observed, good *human* material. Before we begin to train the supernatural life we must try to train a normal, well-balanced individual. Grace builds on nature, and where nature is inferior in urbanity and culture, grace will ordinarily not supply for these disadvantages. Those therefore who seek refuge in the religious life from the conflicts of the outside world, those who were brought up in a Jansenistic twilight of fear, can never really learn to devote themselves fully and generously to a community. What will usually happen is that the individual life of the person will be submerged in that of the community, where all is determined by rule and custom. What should have been a technique of spiritual development becomes in the end a protective coloration for the thin-skinned who seek refuge from the world.

The community must realize that its purpose is to help itself and the individual to grow in love of God and man. In this way each will realize his personal vocation. Every member of the community must be actually given up to it in charity and at the disposal of the other members in genuinely warm familial affection. Otherwise personality will coil back upon itself and selfishness and passivity will develop.

One is often told, especially by European Catholics but to some extent by Americans, that many hesitate to enter religious life these days for fear they will lose that objective contact with reality, that independence of thought and judgment, and that ability to assume responsibility which they had in the world. They fear, in short, a loss of those personal values which they have cultivated at great cost and which they believe to be morally desirable. It is the task of a wise and truly Catholic community to prevent such losses through revitalization of the idea and practice of common life.

NOTES

1. A. Grail, "Love of My Neighbor," in *Love of Our Neighbor,* ed. A. Plé (Springfield, Templegate, 1955), p. 11.
2. C. Truhlar, *Problemata Theologica de Vita Spirituali* (Rome, P.U.G., 1960), p. 139.
3. *Ibid.,* p. 141.
4. R. Gleason, *Christ and the Christian* (New York, Sheed and Ward, 1958), p. 53.
5. D. H. Salman, "The Social Psychology of the Common Life," in *Communal Life* (London, Blackfriars, 1957), p. 273.
6. W. Bier, "Examen psychologique," in *Vie Spirituelle Supplément* (1954), pp. 118–151; see also Bier, "Practical Requirements of a Program for the Psychological Screening of Candidates," *Review for Religious* (1954), pp. 13–17. Cf. *Review for Religious* (1953), pp. 291–304.

The Process of Growth

2 The Process of Growth

For many religious the word adaptation has an ugly sound. It seems to suggest a disguised attack upon those ancient traditions of their order which incarnate the original spiritual intentions of their founder or foundress. Nevertheless, adaptation to modern conditions is a necessity for every religious congregation if it is to continue to meet the needs of the modern mind.[1]

The Church herself provides a striking example of how this adaptation is to be carried out. Although her doctrine is immutable, she does not hesitate to adopt new formulas to express it, and although she never alters her moral principles, she does develop them in accordance with the spirit of the time. She may modify or alter entirely venerable disciplinary decrees formulated in the subapostolic age. One has only to think of how the regulations concerning fast and abstinence, once so stringent, have now been tempered, or how the eucharistic fast has been recently modified. The changes also adopted by the Church in the reading of the breviary make it evident that she intends to modernize the recitation of the office in certain respects.

Moreover, the Church herself has sometimes nudged religious institutes along the path of adaptation. For example, she has granted a great extension of personal liberty in the choice of confessors for religious, apparently regarding this change as a reasonable consequence of the abandonment of that rigid seclusion which once shrouded many convents and monasteries. Moreover, the twentieth-century legislation concerning frequent communion is an instructive model of the Church's principle of adaptation. When Pius X issued his revolutionary directives in this matter many religious protested, yet they were unable to shake his serene determination to adjust the Church's practice and discipline in this regard. The Church too has led the way in granting to students dispensations from choir, even in those orders in which it is a normal form of life. The medieval popes may have wanted all religious to pronounce solemn vows and practice papal enclosure, but the Church today has granted to many religious societies the right to live outside community life.

In liturgical matters too, while discouraging brash enthusiasts who would reconstruct the liturgy on their own initiative, the Church herself has in certain cases led the way in a return to a purer and more primitive ritual. The restored Easter liturgy is the most remarkable case in point.[2]

Adaptation flows, in fact, from the very nature of religious orders, just as it is part of the practice of the Church herself. A religious group is a living member of the Mystical Body, and as such is subject to the laws which govern all living organisms. Movement, growth and change are necessarily part of the religious life, as they are manifestations of all life. The Church has never pinned her whole hope or faith upon passing forms of devotion or the shifting patterns of temporal existence. Pius X, who was not revolutionary in temperament, maintained that it was necessary for the Church to be pliable and to accommodate herself within reason to the new demands which society makes of her. If she is to leaven the world, she must be aware of its conditions and, without any mitigation of doctrine or moral principles, she must adjust herself to these social realities. Pius XI sounded the same note in his encyclicals on atheistic communism. For he observed that in order to rebuild the social order the Christian must adapt to every-day needs those guiding principles which have been set forth by the Church in the past.[3]

Prudence and caution are, to be sure, required in planning and applying those new methods which adapt the apostolate to contemporary life. And yet the Church affirms that these methods should be tried out, with the requisite caution, especially since modern economic and social questions have become so complicated, and since the external organization of the world is so different from what it was in the past. Principles must be realized in terms of the varying conditions of time, place and culture, and in this way genuine progress will be made.

When the Church acts upon this sort of inspiration she manifests her genuinely incarnate nature, at once immanent to present-day society and transcendent to it. As a result, the Christian cannot coolly withdraw from the world. His task is to engage actively in permeating that world, and his own particular milieu, with the spirit of Christ. There is no moment in time and no particular historical culture to which the saving grace of Christ the Redeemer is alien.

What is required is that the Christian channel this grace of Christ to all such cultures. It is for this reason that the Church has made temporary or permanent modifications even in ancient points of discipline in order to answer the needs of later times and places, and by so doing she has set her seal of approval on that fundamental requisite of all living organisms—adaptation. Religious orders, therefore, in imitation of this divinely guided organization the Church, should adapt themselves according to those very principles employed by the Church.

The fact is that adaptation is simply forced upon the religious of today. It always involves a certain degree of risk, and it is obvious that hard-headed prudence is required if it is to be fruitful.

Since it is often difficult to revoke a change once it has been introduced, and frequently its unfavorable effects can be known only through experience, no change should be made until all the aspects of a situation have been considered. Moreover, it is psychologically impossible for changes to be introduced suddenly without causing shock, and at times disorientation, on the part of the community. Often, too, these changes not only produce consternation but also give evidence of a certain spirit of unrest, with the result that the less well-balanced members of the community, seeing one change made, decide upon their own initiative to introduce others.

Experimentation is extremely desirable before a permanent change is made. If a temporary expedient is introduced which seems to be unwieldy, or to produce a condition less desirable than the previous state of affairs, then another experiment of a different character can be made, until by trial and error one has found the most suitable means to the end desired. In this way no "permanent" changes will be introduced which must be revoked later.

Frequent consultation with members of other communities will prove helpful with regard to projected changes. Advice should be sought not only from members of one's own institute but also from those of other institutes who have engaged in the same type of work and have coped with the same sort of problem. And it is, of course, the part of wisdom to seek advice from members of the community whose experience in certain details may be broader than that of the local or general superior. Nor should such consultation be limited to those conservatives who are known to oppose all innovation.

In order to adapt observances and customs one must begin with a clear understanding both of that ideal of the particular institute which adaptation is to serve and of the specific demands of the age which make adaptation imperative.

Unless one can discern the difference between the essential spirit of the institute and its incorporation in concrete details the task of adjustment is impossible. At times it may seem that the modification of one or other detail will involve some impoverishment of the basic spirit. Hence we must have a sure concept of what constitutes the nucleus of an organization and its tradition, and we must be able to distinguish this perennial spirit from its delimitation in the literal observances of the law.

It is possible for a living organism to develop according to a precise law and to gather to itself the material necessary for its own fulfillment. But for a religious body to do this, there must be a clear understanding of the reason for its particular existence and its particular apostolate. Obviously the founder, guided by the Holy Spirit, crystallized in certain rules the order's central inspiration, but these rules are not all of equal importance. Certain rules which deal with the broad outlines and the aims of the institute, its fundamental aspirations, are of greater importance than those which deal with precise material details. Hence adaptation should be begun by an over-all consideration of the purpose of the institute, the particular form of communal life, and the apostolate to which it is directed. The external rules which express and incarnate the particular spirit of an institute contribute to the stability of the organization. The more general principles of law usually will not need to be changed, since they are formulated in terms broad enough to meet the needs of any soul in any age. It is the secondary element which will require change, the details, which should be brought up to date and which in general can undergo modification without harm to the spirit.

For example, in certain religious orders, when the superior points out a defect in religious observance, the subject kneels, waits until the rebuke is administered, kisses the floor and then proceeds to a lengthy and rather elaborate formula of repentance. There is something beautiful and gracious about this stately medieval observance. But obviously what it is intended to express, according to the spirit of the institute, can be accomplished in other ways. The courtly customs which obtained, for example, in seventeenth-century France or medieval Italy do not commend themselves to modern youth. However, the fact that modern youth employs other formulas of courtesy does not mean that it lacks the essence of courtesy. It prefers rather to embody this fundamental inspiration in formulas which do not seem over-abstract, stilted, conventional or artificial. Hence, it is possible that in these more concrete details of observance a certain distance can be travelled towards accommodating the modern outlook to the original ideal which constitutes the spirit of the law. If this is not done, small details which have been allowed to continue long after their usefulness has ceased can become wearisome and distasteful.

It is clear, too, that along with prudence a certain amount of decision and firmness is required for adaptation. Prudence does not mean inertia, nor does it require such protracted delay that a practice is not interred until years after its usefulness has perished. Once a practice has been recognized as inhibiting rather than fostering the purpose for which it was introduced, it should be changed without delay. Otherwise a certain festering restlessness can weaken the religious community which knows itself to be living by outmoded and even ridiculous forms producing effects exactly opposite to those originally intended.

Superiors will at times have to point out clearly, especially to older subjects who are accustomed to certain procedures, that these are not essential to the spirit of the institute and that the new customs should be embraced with generosity and alacrity. The principle that what was good enough for our fathers is good enough for us should not be supported. The apostolate must be kept in mind, and the mind must be kept open.

It is well to remember the natural tendency of human nature to install itself comfortably in a routine to which it is accustomed, even if that routine appears on the surface more difficult and more laborious than the new one suggested. The advantages of routine should not be defended purely on the basis of routine. There is a difference between custom and divine tradition; there is a difference also between custom and the fundamental tradition of an order, and this difference should be pointed out clearly to subjects.[4]

Unless this is done, it is likely that religious orders will continue to experience great difficulty with modern subjects. They will also experience difficulty in the recruitment of new vocations. As a matter of fact, many of the older religious orders are encountering such difficulty today. At times the newer institutes and the missionary institutes flourish while the older religious families have extraordinary trouble carrying on their many activities. It is also occasionally true that the missions of an order or a congregation manifest vitality while the houses back home languish and attract few or no vocations.

Young persons of today look for certain values in the religious life. They frequently feel that the forms of the life of perfection which have been founded and approved more recently offer a more congenial atmosphere, one with which they have an intuitive sympathy. They believe that the older orders tend to smother personalities under a sandpile of traditional and arbitrary details.

It has sometimes been noticed that recruits to the older orders, or to those which have not systematically adapted their spirit to contemporary realities, suffer acute nervous tension, with subsequent loss of vocation. Today's youth are quite different from those of a generation ago. There is at present, psychologists tell us, a far more widespread emotional instability than our ancestors knew. In America, for example, one out of every ten youths needs some kind of psychological or psychiatric counselling to unravel the problems which the pressure of today's tense world creates for him. Doctors have also noticed that young people show less nervous resilience than those of a generation ago. The tension interlacing the contemporary civilization in which our youth has been formed undoubtedly puts enormous strains on nervous energy.

There are also certain ideas in the air which contribute to a more restless, irritable, and frequently critical spirit. As most spiritual directors have noticed, young people of today are preoccupied with the idea of self-development. They wish to know in precise detail what the religious discipline under the particular form which they have embraced is going to contribute to their spiritual and intellectual maturation. They do not easily accept the possibility that they may be intellectually or spiritually maimed as a result of this same religious formation. Nor do they accept the idea that their personality is to remain for many years that of a small child.

This does not mean that generosity is not as much present in most young people today as it has ever been. The character of today's youth is the product of a variety of formative influences in modern society.

First, there is the factor of education. Today's youth have been trained since early school days to adopt a critical and scholarly approach to problems. They are used to weighing their own opinions and to discussing and debating these ideas with professors. The prevalence in the schools of seminar methods, of group discussions, of what is called "democratized education" makes it evident that modern youth finds it difficult to repress personal convictions and to accept authority from another without question. Moreover, it is quite possible that many who enter religious orders today have actually received a better education from a formal point of view than have those who are appointed to train them in that order. This is almost an inevitable consequence of the progress of education.

In their social life also, today's youth have experienced a greater degree of freedom than was permitted to previous generations. Very often they have led for years, before entering religion, a life under their own initiative marked by the power to take decisions, to calculate responsibilities, to administer funds and to conduct themselves as adults. It may be that before entrance they have been active and zealous members of lay organizations, such as Catholic Action, in which they have developed a spirit of initiative and leadership as well as a spirit of community action. Justly proud of their formation as lay Christians, they do not intend to allow the religious life to destroy the very qualities which contributed so much to their apostolate in the modern world.[5]

In addition to these factors of education and experience, the atmosphere of the modern world tends to develop virtues quite diverse from those of earlier generations. In the past, devout youth was characterized by a strong sense of duty; much emphasis was placed on the virtues of docility, modesty, obedience. The spiritual training which young people encounter today appears rather to foster self-development, self-fulfillment, what are thought of as more positive virtues, with the inevitable result that docility, modesty, and obedience have been somewhat downgraded.

People in the world today are troubled by factors in the religious life which seem to them artificial or restrictive of the full development of a spiritual personality. Much of the non-essential apparatus appears trivial, conventional or childish even to sincere and humble aspirants. The idea that in entering the religious life they may be shorn of the initiative developed by life in the world is naturally repellent to them unless the supernatural reasons for the necessary elements of community life are very clearly explained. All these conditions combine to present superiors with a problem of adaptation.

Doubtless one must be very careful in the selection of candidates. Frequently the new psychological examinations mentioned in the foregoing chapter will help to decide which candidates have the emotional maturity and spiritual balance to attempt a religious life.[6] But even in the case of an ideal candidate, those who are concerned to continue the work of their institute should understand that a twentieth-century man or woman often feels stifled in an atmosphere designed for the seventeenth century. They must attempt to understand the needs of the vocations that God sends us today.

Superiors, for example, should make all allowances for the educational factor and not expect the university-trained student to react in the same fashion as a girl from a farm or a boy who has never known the college or university atmosphere. Our young people who have learned early in life to cope with certain problems without consulting others feel that they should have some measure of independence in the religious life also. The abilities which they have developed should not be wasted. For the most part they are open-hearted, and when presented with high ideals and an explanation of how these are related to practical life they are responsive to direction which yet allows scope for initiative.

Today's Christian desires to discover Christ in all things

and to retain a respect for natural values. Anything which seems like hypocrisy, insincerity or artificiality and conventionality distresses him extremely, and this applies to certain forms of piety adapted to a previous generation. He finds himself stifled by a rule which makes his life too monotonous and too dependent upon others. This reaction to monotony becomes a particular trial if the young men or women feel that it is unnecessary. A course of studies, for example, which is ill-suited to them or one far below their capacities leaves them completely confused. That sense of faith our ancestors had, which permitted the young religious to make an act of faith in the intellectual or spiritual training he or she was receiving, no longer prevails. Modern youth reserve faith for divine truths; they want to have human procedures explained to them intellectually so that they can judge and criticize.

All these qualities can be utilized by skilled superiors. The intelligent youth who dislikes routine can be trained to be resourceful in thought and action. The critical spirit developed by his education has most often equipped him with a sensitive, inquiring intelligence, courageous in coping with intellectual and spiritual issues. This can be of great advantage to his order. Although he may perhaps have too much respect for his own liberty, he has at the same time an idealistic desire to avoid the mediocre, and if this is properly directed it can open up avenues of sanctity. Frequently, too, he feels that he is much more mature than he actually is, and the theoretical explanation of things he advances is only a cover for his inexperience. This presumption can be rooted out by kindness and firmness. In general he is open, frank, without duplicity—and in this he some-

times has an advantage over the preceding generations who
were trained to docility at any cost.

Religious superiors who have made a special study of the
sociological and psychological conditions under which the
modern mentality is formed will be capable of guiding
youth, and youth will recognize in them an understanding
spirit. Older religious must be brought to realize the changes
which have taken place. If the religious superior actually
understands his or her subjects, he or she will be able to
guide and instruct them in such a way that they will respect,
admire and follow his or her advice. He or she should be
ready to listen to young people's problems and their solu-
tions for them without judging impatiently that these so-
lutions are immature, owing to a lack of experience. It is an
admirable thing to encounter, as one often does, very old
religious who have a complete grasp of the contemporary
spirit and who are able to use the modern idiom in communicating eternal truths to their subjects. Such a superior
readily wins the affection of youth, whose generosity will
then lead them to follow his or her direction.

The observance of the rule should not crush the young
subject. If it is a hindrance rather than a help, it would be
better in some cases to modify by dispensation certain
practices until the young religious matures sufficiently to
fulfill all the details of the religious life with joy and perfection. Heroic fidelity to the regulations of the religious order
is necessary if adaptation has not made their significance
readily accessible. Youth should be trained to understand
the purpose of certain regulations and not to regard them as
artificial or unnecessary without examining their history and
their function in the order. On the other hand, superiors

should avoid attributing an *absolute value* to individual rules which are, after all, only a means to the end envisaged by the founder or foundress. Love for the spirit of the rule should be inculcated at all costs. Doubtless young subjects must be trained to obey even when they cannot understand the reasons for it, but, ordinarily speaking, superiors should not be loath to explain and to defend observances, customs and rules.[7]

Today almost everyone is convinced of the necessity of adaptation, and yet all too frequently conservative religious orders move very slowly in that direction. It may be necessary at times for a superior-general or a superior to explain to the subject that adaptation is not a problem which involves only the present day, nor is adaptation necessarily a deterioration. If one knew the history of the order thoroughly, one would discover that previously, in times of social ferment, it made certain changes, and that it is necessary that the religious life be adjusted to new circumstances of time just as it is necessary that young religious adjust themselves to a preformed way of perfection in the institute. It should be emphasized that adaptation has gone on as long as the Church has been in existence. If it is conducted with prudence, discretion and dispatch, one has nothing to fear, and this attitude should be induced in the older and the younger religious alike.

It is obvious, for example, that a person in the classroom who does not know how to adapt his way of speaking to the various degrees of intelligence represented there will not be successful. It is simply the intelligent application of the principles of psychology which demands that we make particular adjustments to particular circumstances. A living being incapable of adaptation is doomed to death. In the same way, an apostolate which is incapable of adaptation is itself doomed. This is a universal law, and we are not evolutionist when we adhere to it.

Religious life imposes obligations and norms of conduct which in some ways are reflections of the special period or epoch at the time of their foundation. These items of frozen history can and should be adjusted to meet modern circumstances. For example, the religious habits of many orders of women were originally the garment of the poor of a particular section in a particular country. They were chosen simply because they were completely acceptable to the period, country and class. Hence one wonders why this same habit is clung to today when it has become greatly at variance with the modern dress of the ordinary woman of any particular country or class in society.

Often religious object to the idea of adaptation because they are firmly convinced that it means some change for the worse in the basic principles of the spiritual life taught by the Church and the founder of the religious order. This is clearly mistaken. The bed-rock principles of the ascetical life remain intact and must remain intact forever. It is their application to certain circumstances which may change. Adaptation is not soft pedagogy for weak souls but sound pedagogy designed to lead strong souls more effectively to the love of God, the neighbor and the apostolate of the particular order. One will never abandon prayer, self-abnegation, charity or love of one's rules. The religious spirit will always be opposed to that spirit of relaxation, selfishness and worldliness which is characteristic of an unchristian milieu.

The family spirit of each institute too is always something which must be jealously guarded, but one must be careful to distinguish its authentic spirit from an antiquated letter. This is no easy task, but one requiring a genuine and thorough understanding of the reciprocal relationship between the two. The founder had a definite purpose in mind when he established his organizations, and the rules are the first statement of that spirit. They defined and incorporated it. But tradition and customs of lesser importance generally tend in time to grow up along with the essential regulations of the order. Certain pious practices which attract the religious of one generation may become incorporated by tradition into a rule of conduct for subsequent members of the organization. Sometimes this rich accumulation of customs and ways which are not essentially bound up with the spirit of the order can risk defeating the fundamental tradition itself.

Normally speaking, the carrying out of the law should not stifle the spirit. The law should itself be an incarnation of the spirit, giving it body and substance and clearly defining it. Because man is made up of body and soul it is perfectly normal that certain external observances, gestures and customs should be used to express and prolong a state of soul which the rules strive to obtain. And yet if the natural balance between body and spirit is upset, if the gesture is no longer a spontaneous and normal one corresponding to the intention of the rule, it can be dropped. It is quite possible to make certain changes in the letter of the law without killing the spirit. Admittedly, the letter is necessary to the existence and embodiment of the spirit and is of value insofar as it helps to express it. Yet Christ Himself and all His saints have warned us against confusing the two. Observances which fail to evoke the spirit for which they are intended become useless and burdensome to the soul. Consequently, a very careful study must be made properly to subordinate the letter to the spirit and to avoid ritualism and legalism.

Those who are called upon to instruct young religious should insist upon the dangers of formalism and of putting trust in outward observances of the rule. The great unchanging principles of the spiritual life can be embodied in different outward forms, and in fact the constitutions of religious institutions are not infrequently revised by the congregations or orders themselves. All intelligent law admits of adaptation and of revision designed to deepen its true purpose.

Some adaptations to the law are, as we have noted, forced upon religious by the Church herself. This is obvious, for example, with regard to certain customs of long standing in the religious life. In many cases of women's congregations particularly, it was the custom for the religious to receive communion in order of seniority. At the suggestion of the Congregation of Sacraments, much more freedom has been given to abstain from holy communion, and this freedom has been facilitated in many religious orders by dropping the custom of approaching the holy table in order of seniority. Other changes are forced upon the institute by reason of its own growth. When, for example, a religious order founded in one country spreads to another it is frequently necessary to make certain changes and adaptations in details of clothing and housing. It should be equally evident, therefore, that the changes in modern youth call for similar adaptation in the religious community.

Since the demands that education makes upon us today are so much greater than in the past, our professional equipment should be correspondingly better, and this requires proper training and atmosphere. The Juniorate is highly advisable for all those sisters who are to be engaged in any type of educational work. Its establishment will doubtless be a sacrifice for the first few years, but it should be incorporated or at least planned for immediately.

Moreover, the religious formation of brothers, priests and sisters should take a definitely more doctrinal turn. The mistress or master of novices should present the theology of the ascetical life during the postulancy and the noviceship in a thoroughly doctrinal manner. Principles, concepts and ideals should be expounded with the aim of fostering solid Christian virtue and not mere piety or devotion, much less sentimentality. This obviously requires an instructor whose own formation has been soundly theological. A training of this sort is now provided by certain schools of theology which offer to sisters and brothers the possibility of obtaining degrees in that field of learning. The theological principles which guide the spiritual life should not be taught in a dryly speculative fashion, but neither should their speculative development be omitted nor their historical dimensions ignored. Young people should have some appreciation of the unfolding of an idea through the centuries, and they should realize that there are characteristic family emphases given those concepts by the different schools of spirituality.

Above all, there must be an active and practical participation by the young religious during these noviceship classes. They should be urged to propose their own difficulties and to ask questions. This will nourish those qualities of independence of judgment and that love of reasonableness, sincerity and individual responsibility which can contribute so much to the formation of mature personal convictions. From time to time the novices should be interrogated on their intellectual understanding of spiritual principles, and an intellectual understanding should be demanded. One should not be satisfied with a purely devotional exposition of some topic. The youth of today, as we have observed, aspire to personal initiative and are profoundly realistic. This should be encouraged, and their attitudes of sincerity and generosity should be mirrored by a sensible spirituality that makes allowance for individual differences which it does not stifle or crush but shapes and develops.[8]

Intelligent superiors can help generous young people understand and willingly accept certain factors in the religious life which at first seem opposed to the full development of personality. If a novice has been shown the full theological dimensions of the notion of obedience, he or she will more easily perceive that obedience is not simply a question of human prudence but an infallible method of guiding the soul towards God. Many young people today even complain when they cannot find a rule austere enough to satisfy their aspiration for total commitment of themselves to God. Yet the spirit of initiative which they have developed in today's world, with its cult of personality, makes it difficult for them to yield their wills in obedience. Sometimes the trouble is that they have never been instructed in the genuinely theological concept of obedience and believe that it is based upon some kind of natural leadership, or that it represents the will of the majority. Hence if the superior educates them carefully and directs their attention to the supernatural nature of their vocation, it will often be easier for them to obey. This is particularly true if the superior is intelligent enough to recognize differences in talent and character and does not treat all his or her subjects alike.

Superiors should avoid giving orders which are intentionally absurd, to try the subject's spirit of obedience. This form of pedagogy does not appeal to the modern mind and is little calculated to have the effect intended. Naturally, superiors should avoid suggesting that their decisions appear, to themselves at least, as the immediate and infallible inspirations of the Holy Spirit. Modern youth is sensitive to any hint of tyranny in the attitude of those who wield authority. Government by law and not by arbitrary whim wins their respect. Justice and kindliness, without condescension or the assumption of superior knowledge, will often be more effective than a direct attempt to control the will of the subject. Moreover, people today are repelled by the naive enthusiasm which proposes all superiors as fonts of wisdom in the natural order. It is even more repugnant when these superiors themselves confidently assume that they have a charismatic competence in such natural disciplines as science, literature, and art when their competence is actually severely limited.

That blind obedience which was occasionally appealed to in the past for the vigorous exercising of spiritual neophytes ought to be rarely employed, since it is likely to have an effect precisely the opposite to that intended. It is more likely today to foment discord than to inculcate docility. Consequently, it should not be proposed as the normal expression of obedience. It is not contrary to the theology of obedience if a superior explains the reasons for his decisions.

This is not always possible, but when it can be done diplomatically it will be a help.

The externalism and the formalism characteristic of much religious life today, particularly among nuns, should quite definitely be eliminated. All too often mistresses of novices have insisted upon an external observance, discipline and regularity which produce a type of pious conformism insufficiently related to the ultimate goal of religious life: the development of one's union with God and the apostolate. The rule itself should not be canonized into an absolute and ultimate norm of action. The rule is not holy in itself but leads to holiness insofar as it fosters that interior holiness which counts before God. It would be gross legalism to propose the rule independently of this interior attitude, or to extol it as though it were an absolute, fallen directly from heaven without need of development, interpretation or adaptation. Unfortunately, as we have already noted, many of the smaller details of our observance in religious life have today lost their aptitude for interior sanctification. One notices, for instance, the excessive formalism implied by the practice of ritual bows to the superior, or the convention which prescribes a special place for the superior in the chapel. Many of these antiquated ceremonials should be speedily dropped. The law has a function, and its fulfillment, if rightly motivated, is conducive to a great development of the interior life, but legalism is clearly inimical to a religious spirit.

At times the observance of the minutiae of the rule is forced upon religious with excessive rigidity. Religious are presumed to be adults, and adults ought not be obliged to seek permission for the minor business of life in a convent.

It is a question again of rules which were appropriate to certain historical contexts but are meaningless in the cultural and temporal framework of the twentieth century. Pius XII has pointed out that usages of this sort, if they were ever significant, are nothing but obstacles to a generous vocation once they have become alien to a newer cultural context, and consequently should be dropped. True, some of these rules may have been written by the founder or foundress of the religious order, but, as we have said, fidelity to his spirit means that one adapts his basic inspiration to more concrete circumstances in which alone it can be realized.

The work which religious engage in today requires a spiritual constitution which is vigorous and mature. The modern religious must be competent to think for himself and to exercise reasonable initiative. He should be encouraged therefore, in his formative years, to produce new ideas, to develop seasoned judgment by occasional practice, and to offer suggestions to the community as a whole. Obedience which is ordained to personal sanctification and the organization of a common life is not intended to keep the subject in a state of childishness.

Besides, an excessively formalistic spirit can gradually draw a group further and further away from the life of the people, particularly the poor people to whom they are supposed to minister. Since this is obviously undesirable, the regulations of a community should be streamlined to enable the religious to work with the needy and to be understood by them.

There must also be a certain relief from the tension which the religious life itself engenders. At times women superiors neglect to take this into account, apparently believing that grace will supply for their own lack of the principles of psychology. Work engenders tension, but what engenders it more than anything else is the unconscious conflict which is stoked when one is forced to do things which seem formalistic or even ridiculous.

The daily life of many religious is far too excited and hurried. Superiors should not take on other works which make the daily order even more feverish. There must be periods of calm and privacy. Some attention should be given to programs of normal and legitimate recreation provided by the institute itself. At least, the religious should have adequate time to eat and to rest, there should be certain days consecrated to relaxation, and there should be a summer vacation for everyone. Frequently this need is ignored completely, or Sunday is appointed the day of rest and then devoted to finishing all the tasks which have not been accomplished by the exhausted sister during the week.

Poverty itself suggests that the religious should be rid of anything that is peculiar or extravagant. Starch, pleats and layers of fabrics can be eliminated and the habit streamlined for efficiency, while modesty is preserved. The poor cannot afford to dress in yards and yards of expensive material. (Possibly the elimination of swathes of unnecessary clothing will be not only more hygienic but more conducive to austerity in diet!) Anything that seems odd or strange in religious dress ought to be abolished. Moreover, one should give realistic consideration to the fact of climate. It is a tribute to the spirituality of certain groups of nuns that they are seen in the tropical summer characteristic of most of North America, proceeding calmly about their work encased in layers of serge or other heavy wool. It is, however, no tribute to the common sense of the superiors to permit this. Winter clothes and summer clothes ought to be different, and even the poor are able to manage it.

It is required in certain institutes that the habit be made of specified material now so expensive that it could under no circumstances be considered a mark of religious poverty to wear it. In such cases the specifications should simply be changed, and the habit should be made of poorer, more common material. It is well known, too, that some religious whose house-habit is especially picturesque have another, more sober one to wear outside. It is quite possible that more religious could modify and simplify their street garb. Many religious priests who wear a distinctive, even medieval, habit within a monastery wear a "clergyman" or suit when they emerge. Perhaps religious sisters could adopt an analogous modification. There are today groups of religious who wear ordinary street dress when they are not living in their community, and it would be advantageous were this custom to spread. In many cases the spirit of poverty would endorse some such arrangement, since the arguments which are usually offered in defense of a highly distinctive habit cannot be urged successfully in every instance. At any rate, religious habits should always be modest, simple and hygienic.

The cultural formation of religious should not fall below that of those with whom they are expected to work. The apostolate demands that religious know something of the cultural life of the times in addition to their Christian heritage. It is not particularly edifying if a priest or sister is totally ignorant of the fine arts. Neither is it edifying to observe religious formations which result in an absolute inability to do any independent reading or studying.[9]

Superiors should encourage their subjects to discuss adaptation with them in an open and frank way, and they should not keep from them publications which encourage adaptation. They should be willing to consider candidly anything which will foster the work of the institute and lead to greater interior sanctity. The institute will remain viable only if it remains open to influences which will enable it to affect the outside world more fully. The ultimate norm of sanctity is not conformity to the holy rule but love of God and our neighbor, as every ascetical theologian has pointed out. As we have repeatedly emphasized in this chapter, we should preserve the positive values in the rules without absolutizing their particular application.

For example, interior detachment from material things more perfectly reflects the spirit of Christian poverty than sheer indigence does. Luxury should be ruthlessly eliminated, but those things which greatly assist the apostolate should be incorporated. A superior who provides this sort of formation will be able to explain the customs of an order intelligently to those who are interested in entering it.

Many young girls today find it quite incomprehensible that a nun may not eat with another nun of a different congregation. They also find it unintelligible if they are told that sisters may not visit the home of their parents although they may visit with them if they sit outside the house in a parked car. Yet this does not mean that such girls are unsuitable candidates for the convent. What kind of a convent, indeed, would it be which valued the docile and conventional religious or the pious conformists above those wise and mature enough to want to understand the future of the institute? [10]

There are other adaptations which we might speak of concerning details of the religious life. Poverty, for example, needs to be conceived according to the apostolate in which a particular group is engaged. This point has been touched upon above, but we advert to it again in some detail. Machines, typewriters, telephones, thermo-fax, duplicating machines of all sorts are quite compatible with strict religious poverty if they are required to make the work more efficient. It is inefficient and wasteful to employ talented men and women in tasks which could be done by a machine in a few minutes. One wonders, at times, what business men and efficiency experts would think if they were to explore the use to which religious put their talents and their time. Obviously, the religious does not perform his or her work with efficiency as a chief consideration. Nevertheless religious men and women require means of support, and in the modern world they can no longer rely on the generosity of a few great families. They must therefore organize their work to bring in the necessary amount of food and to provide proper living conditions.

So far as the table is concerned, care should be taken that food be sufficient to nourish the individual and enable him to do his work. There are convents in which the quality of the food is so poor and its nutritional value so low that one wonders how the sisters are expected to survive, let alone do a day's work—or, as frequently happens, do two or three days' work in one.

When religious men and women are engaged in graduate studies, they should be granted the time and the resources enjoyed by lay people studying under favorable conditions. Thus it will occasionally be necessary to allow them to eat meals outside the convent. A similar lenience should be allowed when they attend conventions. It is ludicrous to send religious to conventions and to demand at the same time that they dissociate themselves from all the informal social aspects of the meeting on the grounds that these involve some deviation from the minutiae of convent life. Instead, the sisters should join their academic associates at the customary teas and banquets.

If a religious is working at a university, it ought not be necessary that each time she visits the library a sister companion should sit idly by. Clearly the rule of companionship should in some cases be modified to allow religious sisters, particularly those engaged in these university studies, to pursue their work under normal conditions.

Finally, certain adaptations are in order for the religious exercises of piety, as they are called. There are prayer practices which tend to produce superficial piety rather than deep religious commitment. Some institutes should provide more opportunity for individual prayer and prune the luxuriant growth of prescribed community prayers. Liturgical prayer should have precedence, but mental prayer should not be suffocated by time-consuming devotional practices and vocal prayers recited in common. The multiplication of vocal prayers served another generation well, but it is unattractive to people who appreciate the necessity for mental prayer and at times find vocal prayers harder to prolong than meditation.

As we have observed, women today usually enter the convent with considerably more intellectual formation than their predecessors of a generation ago possessed. Hence it seems absurd to continue the ancient custom of reading a highly simplified meditation to the entire community at night and in some cases rereading it the next morning. Greater liberty of spirit should be allowed the individual religious in selecting his or her own material for meditation without the aid of "point books," which are often jejune and moralistic in tone. It will be helpful, too, on many occasions to allow religious more freedom to fulfill their exercises of piety in private. There is really no reason why spiritual reading made in private cannot be as profitable as spiritual reading made in common or in public.

So far as corporal penances practiced in religion today are concerned, we should remember that modern constitutions may be less robust and nerves more strained than in the past. Many contemporary religious may do better to exercise penance through work and interior disposition than through external austerities. This must be adjusted, of course, according to the spirit of each constitution. The Holy See, as we have observed, has shown the way here by suspending and adjusting laws of fast and abstinence, and it has done so in view of the pressures imposed by modern man's physical routine. Since the tensions of present-day life frequently leave young subjects nervous and exhausted, it would be better in certain cases to reduce the number of corporal austerities, leading the soul to a greater love of God through interior mortification, and especially through the mortifications inseparable from fidelity to common life.

NOTES

1. Many practical helps to adaptation can be found in the *Religious Life Series* published by Newman Press.

2. J. Creusen, "Adaptation," in *Review for Religious* (1949), pp. 87, 89.

3. Victor de la Vièrge, O.C.D., "The Principle of Adaptation," in *Religious Sisters* (Newman, Westminster, 1954), p. 246.

4. J. Gallen, "Renovation and Adaptation," in *Review for Religious* (1959), pp. 333–335.

5. de la Vièrge, *art. cit.*, pp. 258–262.

6. W. Bier, "Practical Requirements of a Program for the Psychological Screening of Candidates," in *Review for Religious* (1954), pp. 13–17. Cf. *Review for Religious* (1953), pp. 291–304.

7. J. Gallen, "Renovation and Adaptation," in *Review for Religious* (1959), p. 335.

8. de la Vièrge, *art. cit.*, p. 247.

9. J. Gallen, "Renovation and Adaptation," in *Review for Religious* (1959), p. 344.

10. J. Gallen, "Renovation and Adaptation," in *Review for Religious* (1955), pp. 299–305.

Christian Maturity

3   *Christian Maturity*

The religious life aims at a twofold maturity. The first is spiritual maturity, the second, human or psychological maturity, which is related to the first but not identical with it. It is not identical because even in neurotic and infantile characters it is quite possible to find a high development of the theological and moral virtues and a ready susceptibility to the impulses of the spirit. Nevertheless, the ideal spiritual development of man includes a simultaneous growth of spiritual and affective maturity. It is obvious to many concerned with the religious life that at times psychological maturity does not keep pace with maturity of age or spiritual maturity. The question then arises: why is it that one meets so many problem-characters in religion? why does it seem at times as though religious practice and doctrine were themselves creating a milieu unfavorable to mental health? The Freudian explanation is quite simple. Since religion itself is an escapism, a refusal to cope with the difficulties and problems of extra-mental reality, it will naturally both foster and attract neurotic and infantile types.

But this is not a valid explanation, quite apart from being unacceptable to the Christian.[1]

Nevertheless, the problem cannot be ignored. Our faith, which normally serves as an integrating factor in the personality, seems in some isolated cases to prove instead a disturbing element. A certain kind of religious training apparently produces an emotional rigidity or apathy which has a deceptive resemblance to emotional discipline and is sometimes mistaken for it. Then, too, mental conflicts centered on fear or aggressivity, such as scruples, can assume a marked religious coloring. Europeans have long asked why it is that many adolescents undergo a crisis of faith which leaves them with no religious resources, despite the fact that they have received a supposedly thorough religious training. Why is it that in the turmoil of adolescence religion should lose its efficacy at the precise moment it should have been a help in achieving that emotional maturity and integration which would liberate the individual from his unconscious pressures and obsessions with self? Why is fear so strong in many Christians that in spite of the New Testament injunction to be free they develop a compulsive-obsessive behavior marked by hidden aggressivity and open terror before God?

It is evident that nature is built upon by grace and that therefore, other things being equal, it is favorable to man and to the full development of the fruits of the Holy Spirit to have a well-integrated psyche. Now a predominant characteristic of maturity in the psychological order is a sense of balance. This should enable one to realize that his freedom is inserted into the context of concrete reality, history and his own environment and may not therefore be used to the detriment of the social rights of others. His maturity is also made evident by a sense of freedom in dealing with others, with himself and with God, a freedom which is not thwarted either by unconscious tendencies or by blocks in his psychological development.

Although it is easier to observe mental health than to describe it, certain of its components have been evaluated, and it may be helpful to reflect upon them.

A definite autonomy is required before we can speak authentically of adulthood in an individual. Unless he has developed within himself a capacity for self-direction and initiative he has no genuine self-possession or adulthood in the true sense of the word. Hence those elements of the personality and of the subconscious which restrain or necessitate activity prevent the growth of personal autonomy and maturity. The adult person, however, is well adjusted to an adult and social world. For this is required a certain ease in dealing with other human beings—equals, superiors and inferiors. It has often been noted that the neurotic experiences great difficulty in opening himself to others and in establishing genuine, warm, human relationships with them. Rigid in his psychological approach, he is also devoid of the ability to develop new friendships.

Every individual is more or less the product of his environment: the ways of thinking, the traditions, the customs, the intellectual atmosphere in which he has been brought up. But the mature individual should establish for himself social relationships based upon judgments of principle and not upon the social patterns into which he has been born. The relationship of the individual to his parents is of such importance in this connection that it can scarcely be exaggerated. The influence of the parents and superiors whom the child has experienced in the past, kind or authoritarian, creates for him a model of which he cannot easily rid himself in the future: he tends to fashion all future figures of authority in the mold of the parents he knew.[2] Psychologists have noted that many adolescent crises of faith which seize the university student are nothing else than a reproduction of the infantile conflict with parents, the fundamental authority figures.

Neurotic characters generally have a disturbed relationship towards authority. Either they wish to be entirely dominated by someone, believing that they are most obedient when they abdicate the core of their individual personality, or, what is more frequent, they live in perpetual revolt against all authority, which may be more or less conscious, betraying itself in various fashions. In certain characters, too, it is violently repressed and gives rise only to a fear of all aggressive behavior.

The mature individual should feel sufficiently secure to enter into genuine relationships with other persons of every age group. Hence he should be capable of objective judgments with regard to others, neither scandalized by weakness nor ignorant of its possibility in those who represent authority or religious values. As long as undiscovered and uncontrolled emotional patterns formed in infancy still reign in the subconscious, the individual judgments will not be objective and will carry with them an emotional charge bearing little or no relationship to the objective situation of adulthood. To demand that the superior be the perfect model of all the virtues—which one does not incorporate into unity in oneself—is irrational. Yet this is one of the more frequent signs of immaturity in religious. Unfortunately, as soon as the immature religious observes some deficiency of intelligence, judgment or virtue in his superior he is likely to abandon all interest in following his directives. The mature man, on the other hand, recognizes that authority is necessary and accepts it in all the limits of its powers as a directive from God, realizing that the fragile human instrument chosen by God to exercise authority does not automatically become invested with natural qualities he did not have before.[3]

Another criterion of psychological maturity is the degree of rationality with which one guides one's actions. To function maturely requires progressive liberation from the sub-rational aggressive and sexual impulses of the child-world. Consequently, the decisions and the opinions of the adult should not be guided by those instinctive fears or sexual conflicts which have never been overcome by intelligence. Intelligence and spiritual affectivity must take precedence over sensible activity. This does not imply, of course, the elimination of affectivity and the turning of oneself into a rigid and robot-like personality. Such a caricature of self-control or discipline is scarcely attractive. But the adult should be able to integrate his emotions into his personality, keeping them firmly under the control of reason and in contact with objective values. The lack of emotional control usually indicates the presence of underlying psychological problems which should have been solved long before the age of majority. While the capacity to see others as they are, to judge situations as they are, to remain in contact with objective reality even when our emotions are aroused, is characteristic of the adult, the adolescent constantly mingles his dream world with the world of actuality.[4]

The ability to get along well with oneself and to assess one's own abilities and failures objectively is an important characteristic of the adult personality. It is not a sign of maturity, for example, to be thrown into total confusion by the recognition in ourselves of some moral defect. A mature attitude is repentance for sin coupled with renewed and more intelligent effort to grow in grace. This applies also to failures in whatever range of our religious life: teaching, preaching, writing and so on. The tranquil acceptance of failure along with the determination to do one's objective best in the future is a test of maturity. To some, failure in social life, in the religious community or in the task to which they are put seems an intolerable thing. The mature way is to accept oneself as one accepts others, with all the limitations that God and our training have imposed. Since none of us is expert in all fields, failure is a quite normal process in many areas of our human existence. A mature individual can accept this fact without widening the gap between his achievement level and his expectation level. To refuse to enter the pulpit unless one can be the most perfect orator who has ever existed is infantile. Growth in personal autonomy takes place only when one realizes one's limitations of natural gifts, age, training, social position and experience.

If the individual is to outgrow the instinctive conflicts of his childhood, so that his adult reactions will not be merely hidden repetitions of tensions having no existence in the objective order, it is necessary that he should begin to establish a hierarchy among values and desires and to order them by reason. Having chosen by objective consideration, in relation to what he is seeking, a definite line of conduct, the adult should be able to continue in it with perseverance and yet with submission to the realistic circumstances of life. Unlike the child, the adult is not entirely swayed by the climate of opinion around him. Frequently we are told that one of the characteristics of adulthood is the ability to adjust, but adjustment does not mean dereliction of principles or being simply carried along on the tide of common opinion. The adult is capable of searching to find what is objectively the best course of action and persisting in it, however unpopular it may be. This, of course, is not a recommendation for pure stubbornness. Thus "the all or nothing attitude" which is sometimes drummed into young religious by misinformed spiritual guides is disastrous to mental health. The mature man should be able to distinguish relative degrees of importance, so that the absolute is not mistaken for the relative and the essential for the accidental. Lacking a capacity for objective distinction and a sense of the relativity of values, young religious at times manifest a dogmatism and a severity of judgment extraordinarily immature.

Modern psychologists are more and more accenting the fact that affectivity, love and the emotions play an important role in man's life. Most mental diseases, for instance, are based upon an excess or a deviation of emotion. Thus the failure to regularize one's affective functions or their own insufficiency is a primary cause of many mental breakdowns. There are, of course, mentally sick people whose troubles may be said to be intellectual or objective rather than emotional, but as a general rule the intellectual justifications are second thoughts, the basic trouble being found in the affectivity itself, the sphere of the emotions. (A student, for example, is exhausted preparing for examinations and calls this intellectual fatigue. Actually, the fatigue is not due to the intellectual work but is simply a neurotic manifestation of the more or less intense regrets, desires and frustrations accompanying it.)

It is becoming more and more evident, on the other hand, that the normal development of human emotionality or affectivity does not always parallel man's physical or intellectual growth. Because a child has reached the age of reason it does not follow that his affectivity has reached that stage. This process of maturity is rather one of lifetime duration. From a more far-reaching point of view, we might say that the only genuine passage to the adult stage takes place, not when man becomes intellectually mature, but when he enters the domain of unselfish love.

We do not mean by love the discovery of delight, but the recognition of the existence of other men, the capacity to forget oneself in favor of another, the ability to live above the level of the agreeable or disagreeable, the smooth or harsh. For affectivity formulates our response to the real; it is in relation to reality that personality is either fulfilled and liberated by acceptance or mutilated by refusal or revolt. Moreover, a man is judged an adult much more by his reactions to people than by his reactions to things. And it is especially in his reactions to his equals that adulthood manifests itself in the adolescent or in the grown man. We stress this because, psychologically speaking, superiors and inferiors may still be considered as means, that is, as existing in the domain of object.

Although these truths may seem self-evident, it is necessary to mention them, since modern psychologists are insisting upon them so much more than in the past. And we must note also that modern psychologists no longer tend to identify affectivity with sexuality. There is, undoubtedly, a strong link between sex and affectivity, or emotion. Freud has strongly underscored this. But his conception of the area of affectivity was much too narrow, a fact which modern psychology is now recognizing. Jung has made it clear that aggressivity does not easily reduce itself to what Freud thought it was, namely sexual jealousy. In addition, Jung has shown that aggressivity in human nature is at a much deeper level than sex jealousy. Sex jealousy is simply one case of aggressivity, not its source.

On the other hand, that the phenomenon of sympathy goes far beyond the domain of sexuality Max Scheler has strongly emphasized in his book on the nature and forms of sympathy. Sympathy or love is attached to a very intense form of what is called oblativity, the sentiment by which we exteriorize our affection and make an offering of ourselves in unselfish generosity to another. The important thing to remember is that the victory of this unselfish love over infantile or adolescent aggressivity is precisely what constitutes entrance into the full adult state of manhood. When man is capable of forgetting himself for another, then he is a man. Before this he is, psychologically, a child.[5]

These points of contemporary psychology do not appear at first to have a direct interest for the religious life, except for the fact that whatever touches psychology touches education and the practical direction of consciences. But they become more interesting when we realize that the religious life is itself a life and must follow the laws of human life and of human psychology. In particular, there is in the religious life a place for a development which goes from the infantile stage to the adult stage. It is regrettable that many

Catholics never undergo it. By this I do not mean that they do not know the truths of their religion. Actually, they may be learned theologians, yet infantile still in the life of the spirit. What has happened is that their relationship to God on the level of religious psychology is only that of a child, not the childhood of which Christ is speaking when He says "unless you become as little children" but a childhood which Christ calls upon us to surpass. Adulthood in the religious life demands the balance of affectivity and emotions. It implies that one passes from selfish to oblative, or selfless, attitudes. It implies a victory of selfless love over aggressivity in all its forms of conquest or defense. To speak in more traditional terms, the fullness of religion is the passage from fear to love, beyond the attraction of pleasure and the repugnance for the disagreeable, even if these be spiritual.

Yet a certain fear of God must remain. It would be well if those who instruct young religious were to have a firm grasp of the concept of fear of the Lord; there is often great confusion in this regard, since the word fear can cover so broad a variety of emotional and theological areas. One might ask at the beginning the extent to which fear is in time to be integrated into love of God.

First of all there are two quite different types of fear observable with regard to the religious life. That servile fear which essentially consists in the fear of punishments for wrong-doing, the fear of hell and so on, has its main value and efficacy at the beginning of the spiritual life. Its prime value consists, even here, not in the element of aversion or terror but rather in the attachment to the good God from whom we fear to be separated by wrong-doing. This type of fear of God and His punishments is a moral good primarily because it is an initial and preparatory stage of love. The simple passion of fear which is an emotional aversion in the presence of danger or evil should not be too readily endowed with a moral value. The fact that one fears harm to oneself may protect the individual in many situations, but it is obvious that one should not approach God with a type of fear which is mingled with aversion, horror, distrust and disgust. It would be quite clearly a very serious sin to treat God as though He were an evil to be avoided at all costs. Rather what is good about this servile fear of punishment is the initial love implicit in it. We fear God less directly than we fear His punishment. It is the justice of God represented in a particular punishment, whether of hell or of some temporal misfortune, that we fear. Since God Himself is the object of hope and love to the Christian, He should be feared not as an evil but only as the source of justice and of hope and love as well. Servile fear, or the fear of punishment, is the very imperfect beginning of that filial or childlike fear which the Christian should grow into later and which is much more closely allied to love.

It is not easy to establish the perfect unity, the perfect coherence, of servile fear with the theological virtue of hope. The predominant part in our spiritual life should be played by faith, hope and charity, and servile fear should not arrogate to itself the major part of our concern with God or with ourselves. It is difficult to see how a soul dominated by this fear of damnation or of the punishment of God can be said to be rooted in that tranquil confidence in Another, the Saviour, which is the characteristic of Christian hope.

A more fully religious attitude and one more closely in conformity with New Testament revelation is filial fear. Filial fear, which in its essence is not so much what the or-

dinary man describes as fear as what he describes as love, is
an attitude which should become more marked as our union
with God becomes closer. Filial fear is a delicacy in inter-
personal relationships which makes us long not to offend or
in any way encroach upon the area that exists between ourselves, who love, and God, the object of our loving. We wish
in no way to offend God, because in doing so we would be
offending another person whom we long to love with all our
powers. The fear which loving husbands and wives experience when they dread in any way to offend the beloved, not
because of punishment for the offense but because their personal relationship itself would suffer and their love might
diminish, is of this kind.[6]

Filial fear is an immediate religious attitude and one
which, as we have noted, naturally increases with our love of
God, for the more we love, the more we long not to disturb
this relationship or to impair it in any way. It is quite con-
sistent with faith, with fully formed hope and charity, that
we should fear more and more in this relationship. Even
in heaven filial fear will remain, in the sense that while we
can no longer fall away from our love of God it will be trans-
formed into that astonishment at the divine greatness and
divine goodness which is akin to admiration. Hence we are
called upon as Christians to pass from the realm of infantile
psychology, where servile fear is prominent and terror about
salvation is characteristic, to an adult world in which filial
fear will grow as we grow in hope and in charity.

Christ has told us that He has conquered the world. Our
baptism is an initial step on the part of God leading us to
heaven, and redemption is now, as well as to come. Hence
the Christian should live his mature life in tranquillity, trusting in one who is powerful enough to redeem him.

St. Paul expects us to pass from fear of the law to obedience through love. This law of life is the integral realization of that unique command of God: "Thou shalt love the Lord thy God with all thy heart, all thy soul, all thy power." For each individual this entails the forgetting of self, not only through the negative way of mortification and denial of self-love but also through the radical recognition of God as the sovereign Lord. Adult religion demands a positive decentralization and forgetfulness of oneself before God.

But forgetfulness of self is no easy matter, for man is naturally possessive. From the earliest moments of infancy children grasp and hold onto things. It is difficult in the spiritual life also because every religious life begins with an attention to one's self. To lead an interior life one must think often about one's self. One must be recollected, as they say, and indeed all Christian tradition invites us to enter within ourselves, to convert ourselves in order that we may find God. Both possessivity and self-contemplation present a threat to our progress toward the adult stage of religious life. But the greater danger lies in the closing in on one's self. God is in the depths of our soul, and St. Augustine tells us in a masterly fashion that we can find Him there. He is more intimate to me than myself. Nevertheless, I must find God there while avoiding the trap of considering God not as Another, but only as a possession of myself. Hence the great danger in polarizing our entire mental life around ourselves, ignoring and losing contact with the exterior world. This is what modern psychology calls autism, concern with self. It is not necessarily a deliberate, clearly definable selfishness, but it is a form of introversion, and that is contrary to full religious development.

It is here that we recognize the supreme "normalness" of

the Incarnation, wherein God chose to reveal Himself to us as another at the same time that He reveals Himself as the soul of our soul. Christ exists as another with whom we can enter into affectionate relationship in our own way. We can stand before Him. We can confront Him. We can forget ourselves in regarding Him outside ourselves.

There is a further point in this question of the relation of contemporary psychology to the religious life which must be made more precise, and that is the importance attached by many psychologists to the sentiment of guilt. Mental disease, say some, whatever its degree and its form, is a condition having guilt as its foundation. We admit at least, since it is universally accepted by psychologists, that the sentiment of guilt plays an enormous role in the majority of neuroses, frequently to the extent of being the very basis of the neurosis.

It is scarcely astonishing that the evil of sin should reveal itself at times in one's mental life and even in one's body. Consequently the feeling of guilt seems clearly dangerous for man. Nevertheless we Christians know that since sin is a reality the sentiment of guilt is of vital importance in religion. St. John says: "If we say that we have not sin in us, then we lie" (1 John 1: 8). But neurotic guilt has little if anything to do with the strict notion of sin and must be distinguished from it. It is rather an irrational feeling which wells up from the depths of the subconscious, an emotional state composed of many elements, including fear, self-hatred and often even aggressivity.

Certain people never resign themselves to the hard fact that they are sinners. Having been brought up in a pious atmosphere, which may have been somewhat sentimental or even infantile, they experience a profound interior terror, at times leading almost to a denial of their faith, when finally confronted with the fact of sin. (It is not always true, as it is sometimes said, that people abandon their faith because they wish to live an immoral life in tranquility.) It is possible, especially for young people in this crisis of faith, to feel an inability to accept this real event which has shown itself to them in the depths of their being—the fact that they are capable of serious sin. So appalled are they at their readiness to sin in certain situations that they reject the very idea of sin, preferring to close their eyes to the reality.[7]

Actually, a neurosis is the beginning of a separation from reality, while a psychosis is complete disorientation from it. It is here that the morbid world of sin really opens up, with the denial of its existence. At this point, all the avenues of nervous disease and of despair reveal themselves. This is particularly so when the person concerned is of a fine and delicate sensitivity. And if the religious training has been sentimental rather than strong, religious sensibility will begin to lose its balance. Non-Christian psychiatrists, or incompletely Christian psychiatrists, in the face of this disaster, will be tempted to abolish in the conscience of their patients the very notion of sin itself. They will do so convinced that the notion of sin has been revealed as dangerous for this individual, that consequently it is necessary "to break the infernal cycle of self-accusation and self-justification."

Even well-intentioned spiritual directors, by frightening young people, or older people who are psychologically immature, can do them great psychological damage. The harm is not from awakening the notion of sin, but from the fact that the person who instructs about sin is frequently himself psychologically immature and dominated by all sorts of unconscious urges in the direction of sin which he does not dare to recognize as such. These unconscious urges drive him into confusion and mental disturbance when he hears of certain types of sins—especially those of sex—forcing him to lash out at his penitent in a wholly emotional, un-christian and untheological way, simply because of his own emotional instability and insecurity and the terror that these sins incite in him.

It is entirely reasonable to demand that no man should deal with sex instruction unless his own attitudes to it are normal, since he is actually communicating not only knowledge but also personal attitudes. Further, no man or woman should give counsel in regard to sexual sins unless he or she is normal psychologically with regard to sex. For example, if the very mention of sex is such as to throw him into total emotional turmoil, a confessor cannot possibly communicate a rational, Christian, theological attitude towards sin.

Moreover, in areas other than that of sexuality, the spiritual director must be able to distinguish real guilt from its neurotic counterpart. An important distinction to be made is that real guilt is proportioned to the sin committed. If I steal one dollar, I am guilty of stealing one dollar, and I regret this. My regret is proportionate to one dollar. If I steal one million dollars my guilt is greater and my regret is proportionate to that, but it would be neurotic of me to have a feeling of guilt proportionate to the second crime if I had been guilty of the first. Guilt is proportionate to the crime committed; so too should be the sentiment of guilt.

Another important distinction between real guilt and neurotic guilt is this: real guilt attaches itself to a definite object; neurotic guilt attaches itself to no object. When I steal a hundred dollars I have a feeling of guilt because I stole one hundred dollars at a definite place and time and from a definite person under definite circumstances. This is normal. When I feel guilty and do not know why I feel guilty, nor of what, nor against whom, I am neurotic. Obviously, neurotic guilt should be dismissed immediately and with force. It is simply not Christian to cultivate an objectless guilt.

Of course no one of these distinctions is made by psychiatrists who attack the notion of guilt, and therein lies the harm of such psychiatry for the Christian. In point of fact, one cannot repress the sentiment of sin without other harmful effects taking place in the soul. Can one forget, as Nietzsche said, and tranquilly digest one's sins, with no feeling of guilt? Would it be normal to do so? And is not this the precise characteristic of a constitutional psychopath?

Sin for a Christian is quite other than what it is in Freud's analysis. It is at once much more terrible but much more curable too. For the Christian knows his sin, not as a failure to himself, not as a renouncement of an ideal of the subconscious, but as a failure to God, a refusal to accept a personal relationship of love with God.

Sin is against God, the other, with whom we are in a relationship which is normal, that of love. This is what makes the gravity of sin. But it is also what creates the possibility of getting out of sin. According to Freud, sin keeps me in a vicious circle because I punish myself, against whom I have sinned. But as a Christian I know that I have sinned against God, and that God can break the circle by pardoning me. He is another, and He can therefore pardon me. But I know that I cannot pardon my own sin, and therefore all my excuses are in vain. I cannot justify myself because this is an infinite and eternal task. But Christianity teaches that as sin is against another, so justification can come from another, namely, God. Our justice is not our justice. As St. Paul stresses, it is God's justice given to us by God. We are not closed irremediably upon ourselves in our sins; if we confess our sins, God is omnipotent and just and will purify us.

Every neurosis of culpability—in fact, every neurosis—is based upon a failure to forgive one's self. Men are caught and imprisoned by the cruel super-ego, who accuses them without pity and without hope. But men are badly pardoned if pardoned by themselves. It is only in the perspective of a relationship with God as another that man can be genuinely pardoned, and then the inevitable recognition of sin will no longer poison us interiorly. In the Freudian system it is sin and the sentiment of sin that poison one. In the Christian scheme of values the sentiment of sin does not generate this interior poison. Nor does sin recognized before a saving God cause us to despair. We accept our sins and we accept the Saviour who conditions our sins and who frees us from them. Consequently we must always recognize the need to be saved; we cannot save ourselves.[8]

On the other hand, we must realize that it is almost impossible genuinely to recognize sin unless one is certain one can be pardoned. Unless one has evidence that redemption is at hand one does not want to admit that one sins. Before the crucified Christ genuine contrition is possible. The revelation of the gravity of sin, no matter how great, is also a revelation of the mercy of God who destroys sin and makes the scarlet sinner as white as snow. The child who is fearful of his parents will almost necessarily lie, inventing excuses to deceive them even if he cannot deceive himself. But if the child knows that he will be pardoned completely, then he will tell the truth. Once you recognize that you are loved even though you are a sinner, you can afford to be a sinner, to repent, to admit it and to be pardoned.

Christian maturity implies that the individual has fulfilled his expectations and has properly perfected his human tools for human functioning; adulthood implies finished growth, the fulfillment of the conditions and possibilities of human perfection. It cannot be stressed too forcefully that a mature viewpoint about self also enters into one's relationship with God and with others. The man who is at ease with himself has established an inner security and is more likely to achieve normal affective relationships with the deity and with other human beings. Naturally one must view this entire problem in its genetic and evolutionary implications. Maturation, as we have seen, is a constantly developing process involving the dissolution of infantile complexes.

Many children seem to look on God as a being before whom one exercises magical gestures and prayers and from whom one can expect, as a result of these rituals, a certain number of benefits. In other words, they visualize divine providence and their relationship to it as a source of goods. This infantile attitude, frequently met with even in those who have reached the age of adults, is found in some religious. When a child's parental relationships have been disturbed, as we have said, or when he has been a product of a neurotic household or one in which there was emotional instability, even though his vocation is genuine one can expect that he will experience considerable difficulty in facing the objective world realistically. Hence the necessity for examining the family background as far as possible before accepting anyone into religion.

A type of immaturity common among religious is a mistaken concept of unselfishness. Instead of being a genuinely free attitude it is actually the result of unconscious pressures. Thus those in whom aggressivity is insufficiently developed may feel that it is their task in life to give everything and to refuse nothing. Besides the "magic of extremes" which this mistaken concept evokes there is also bound up in it an inability to refuse any request. The basic reason for this is the subjective feeling of culpability which would result, unreasonable though it might be. If one has assumed the role of the most unselfish of men, one will naturally feel an affective insecurity, however unreasonable, if one refuses requests made to one. But this is not to act with maturity. The adult is able to calculate the future effects of his actions, whereas the child lives merely in the present. In any concrete situation the adult should be able to examine the entire significance of the situation realistically and then to make a prudential judgment looking to the future results of his decision. It follows that refusals are necessary at times if one is to live humanly and supernaturally and with inner tranquillity.[9]

The inability to say "No" is frequently a disguise for far less pleasant psychological attitudes than the subject suspects. For example, devotion to others can be a way of imposing a subtle control over them, a form of aggressivity seeking to dominate through its affirmation of charity. Or it may be an affirmation of one's sources of strength implying an excessive value judgment concerning oneself. Above all, it may represent the infantile trait that we have described: the inability to recognize the difficulties which will arise in the future from saying "Yes."

One sees an aspect of this same immaturity in the attitude of those whose viewpoint towards positive law is so ill-conceived that they cannot accept even legitimate dispensations granted by legitimate superiors. Likewise in those who refuse to admit that anything but utter blamelessness and a full realization of the ideal could possibly exist in anyone placed over them in a position of authority by divine providence. Maturity requires openness and receptivity to the object and to new ideas as well as to other personalities. The mature subject should be able to enter into a normal, respectful dialogue with authority, neither avoiding contact nor seeking to impose his own ideas upon it.

The normal adult is able to enter into genuine relationships with a structured group such as his community and is neither withdrawn nor resentful of the other members. He has the ability to evaluate others objectively and to correct his own emotional dreams, ideals and unrealizable aspirations for sanctity as well as his own subjective tastes. Unless a man is at ease with himself, recognizing himself objectively for what he is along with all his defects and virtues, he can never assume this normal and free orientation to others in the community, to authority or to God.

Because of the importance which modern man attaches to this notion of adulthood religious superiors would do well to examine all the means at their disposal for fostering psychological adulthood in their subjects. Since it is commonly admitted that the one characteristic found in all neurotics is infantilism, it should be the aim of superiors to help their subjects in banishing every form of this neurotic conflict.*

Because of the disadvantage which will occur to religious institutes if they do not train their young people towards adulthood, houses of studies in particular should be organized to give some expression to mature man's orientation. It has been noticed by many that the atmosphere of seminaries and houses of formation is at times more or less separated from the world of reality. Obviously the formation given in many of these houses is by necessity extremely theoretical and largely intellectual. But at the same time room must be made for the development to affective maturity of the individual's personal gifts. The individual should be brought to a progressive confrontation with the real world and should learn early how to adjust his theoretical and intellectual principles to the concrete situations in which he will later find himself. Otherwise he will be in the dangerous situation of having definitely committed himself to being a professed religious or a priest before arriving at psychological maturity. It is highly undesirable that the professed religious or the young priest should discover his personal problems only after having made a permanent commitment to the religious institution or to the priesthood.

It has been noted by psychiatrists that young religious often emerge from their professional training insufficiently

* It is surprising, even astounding, to realize that there are still religious communities which completely ignore the resources of modern psychotherapy for their subjects. In such communities, and there are many, the neurotic personality is given no assistance beyond the relaxing atmosphere of a country resthouse. This is obviously something which should be changed with all deliberate speed.

mature. This means that they are forced to struggle for maturity with the combined burden upon them of the responsibilities they have accepted permanently, the pressures of the world into which they have been introduced, and the problems which others bring to them. Often it is at the moment they begin their apostolate to others that their own neuroses are beginning to appear.[10]

It should be obvious that the normal individual begins his existence with many non-free, non-chosen elements composing his intellectual and affective patterns. The influence of his social milieu, the traditions of his class, the opinions of his family, all should be surmounted by the adult so that he can calmly withdraw and make an objective judgment on the values embodied in them. He should then be able to adhere freely and lucidly to the values which he incorporates and accepts as his own, that conscious, freely chosen hierarchy of values and aims to which we have referred as being characteristic of maturity.

An enlightened religious formation will often suffice to prevent the development of neurotic conflicts in young religious. We should remember, however, that the prime element of neurosis is usually at least partly subconscious or unconscious. Consequently moral instruction, exhortation to virtue, and even the good will to attempt virtue will not automatically produce psychological maturity. The effort and the intensity that the subject brings to his attempt to fulfill moral exhortation may even complicate the conflict. Hence, one should recognize that in general the nature of mental illness is practically withdrawn from the free dominion of the subject. Neurotic conditions, of course, admit of all degrees of severity or lightness, but in general it can be said that the individual suffering from a neurotic conflict cannot bring his behavior into line with his aims or the superior's wishes simply by an effort of will. Actually it is a question of the re-education of a fundamental outlook of the entire personality which is at stake here, and this should be recognized in the religious formation.

It is observable at times that the inner conflict which the neurotic experiences disturbs his relationship not only with himself but with others and with God. Such neurotic upsets are likely to manifest themselves in anxiety, infantile dependence, or even the feeling of being persecuted. In general, these are emotional illnesses and must be treated as such.

There is no reason to believe, as some seem to, that there is a higher percentage of neurosis among religious than there is in other areas of the population. Nevertheless, there is little doubt that neurotic symptoms can be observed in the convent and monastery and that certain people do use religion as a means of escape from reality. At times, too, the ritualistic pattern according to which religious formation is pursued can lead to very unpleasant results.

It is obvious that one cannot expect young religious to absorb the spirit of their institute automatically; they must be trained to this. But at the same time the great religious insight of the particular founder must not be narrowed to such legalistic application that the original spirit itself is lost. Although the charismatic ideals of the founder must be concretized in law, the young individual must be taught to seek beneath the law the original moral and supernatural insight of the founder. Otherwise the religious insight is in danger of being lost and replaced by a ritualistic pattern.

The more determined and the more complex the rules become, the more likelihood there is that legalism will creep in to strangle the spirit of freedom.

In teaching habit-formation, one should exclude as far as possible the compelling motif of fear and suggest instead the imitation motif of Christ and love. If this precaution is not observed, attitudes can be induced by religious teachers which are not psychologically healthy. Thus it is possible to observe in some subjects an almost compulsive state, characterized by an obsessional need to repeat certain ritualistic patterns of prayers or behavior. The characteristic factor of compulsive activity is, of course, its lack of freedom and consequently its lack of meritorious values. At times one comes across individuals who are actually thrown into a state of terror at the idea of omitting some of their daily ritual prayers or who feel emotionally disturbed, with strong sentiments of culpability, when they accept a dispensation from fast, abstinence or regular order because of illness. This emotional feeling of guilt suggests that the individual thus legitimately dispensed had been motivated partially by ritualistic compulsion and an obsessional fear rather than wholly by love of God. Such an attitude, of course, is neither healthy nor sufficiently removed from what savors of superstition.

It has been often observed that religious formation seems to generate in some individuals a complex of guilt. This is especially true in the case of adolescents making their first break-through into the adult or other-directed social world, and in that of middle-aged persons beginning to feel the failure of their powers, who are, as a consequence, subject to a certain melancholy characteristic of that period of life. But there are other kinds of persons in whom a religious

formation, instead of producing a genuine sense of responsibility and awareness of the guilt of sin, achieves instead a
type of neurotic guilt.

Neurotic guilt is, as we have seen, ineradicable and without proportion to the wrong committed; it is an irrational
feeling in which fear is a strong element. Unfortunately, religious teachers are not always sufficiently careful in distin-
guishing fear and guilt, and their instructions sometimes
provoke unhealthy reactions in young people. It is obvious
that the emotions of dread and anxiety are not those most
likely to produce a mature and responsible attitude in the
subject. It would be disastrous if fear remained the only
motive for the avoidance of wrong-doing, and even more
disastrous if the individual should remain in constant terror
of God while being objectively without grave sin.

As we have seen, the mature man, accepting the fact of
his sinfulness but trusting in the help of a redeeming God,
is able to acknowledge his concrete faults with the same ob-
jectivity with which he treats deficiencies in the natural
order. Since a failure even in the moral order is not necessarily either total or permanent, our attitude towards it is
an index of our maturity.

If the individual religious is formed gradually towards a
sense of responsibility, he will be enabled to accept realistically the consequences of his decisions, whether they
indicate success or failure. In the social sphere one of the
most dominant characteristics of the adult is his ability to
accept responsibility and to wield it with discretion, neither
assuming those tasks which are beyond his powers nor refusing those which are not.

Normally an individual develops such a sense of responsibility in the work of his own profession and through his familial associations, particularly the relationship of parenthood. Since the religious gives up paternity or maternity, he or she should be brought early to experience responsibility. It would, in fact, be disastrous to leave young religious for long without responsibilities and without individual initiative. Nevertheless it is difficult for the superior to arrange for individual responsibility in the younger subjects. Normally their initiative and their responsibility will be shown primarily in observance of the rules and customs of the house of formation and in their studies. However, it is not an infrequent experience to find an individual easily assuming the responsibilities of an intellectual life, especially on the undergraduate level of the house of formation, and being unable to assume other responsibilities later on. Therefore, it would seem wise to present a wide variety of experience and responsibility to the young religious.

It should be clear, too, that the man who is to be a priest or the girl who is to be a nun should be more adult in the affective and sexual sphere than he who is going to be a good father or she who is going to be a good mother. This means that the religious should ordinarily have well understood his or her sexuality and the wide role that sexuality and affectivity play in his or her entire personality. In other words, his or her sexuality should be integrated. It should not be fixated at a level in which the prime object of affective responses is a narcissistic obsession with self.

Psychological maturity requires that the adult religious be able to enter into normal affective relationships while understanding the parental joys and the sacrifice of sexuality which he or she makes. Hence, the sacrifice of the mar-

ried state should be regarded primarily in terms of the affective responses and not directly as the giving up of sexual
goods. Unselfish love and oblativity help a great deal here
to bring the individual to maturity. He should understand
what he has renounced, and particularly its affective and
emotional compensations, so that he chooses realistically, in
full knowledge of what he is doing, the alternative of celi-
bacy.

The mature man is aware that a choice of one good over
another implies a renouncement. The adult is capable of
making a choice in which he foresees and weighs the goods
on either side. When he has chosen he should be able to
pursue his choice without regret. This is especially important when it is a question of a major choice such as vocation. The individual who chooses a permanent orientation in
life without being sufficiently adult is likely later on to show
an infantile regret that he cannot enjoy both sides of the
choice. This is a characteristic immaturity which we find at
times in religious, who after having made a choice of life
which by its nature excludes certain goods, still hanker
after those of the affective and human order which by the
very nature of the case are denied them.

That which serves as a norm in the ordinary individual
for all human relationships of love is the relationship of
married love. For married love gives to the subject that
reciprocity of affection, that openness and unimpeded ac-
cess to another, and that capacity for self-donation which
is also the foundation for consecrated chastity. Those who
find themselves constitutionally unresponsive to sexuality
are not the most suited to a life of consecrated virginity. The
religious must constantly labor to develop within himself a
capacity for genuine altruistic self-donation to Christ and

His members; otherwise there is danger of spiritual deformation. In such cases chastity can be an ill-concealed form
of sublimation, an unconscious device for avoiding responsibilities, particularly the prime responsibility of achieving
adulthood.[11]

There is one further precaution which should be observed
by the religious educator: the master or mistress of novices
must make the most serious efforts to eliminate from his or
her instruction the tension overtones deriving from a certain
type of moralism. We are all familiar with that kind of religious instruction which represents a morality of duty that
can only be called Kantian. Under whatsoever names and
devout clothes this form of self-sufficient ethic presents itself, it still remains utterly opposed to the entire mystery of
Christianity, which is essentially an epic of love in which
our relationship with God is a communion of personal love
and not merely a morality of obligation or duty. Frequently
the man of obligation or duty may manifest virtues which
in the natural order are highly to be admired, but in their
specific tonality and quality they are stoical rather than
Christian. Since young people are very susceptible to atmos-
pheres and absorb, by a sort of emotional assimilation, the
attitudes of those who teach them, it will do no good for
the master or mistress of novices to inveigh against Christian moralism if he or she is unconsciously infected by this
error.[12]

Christian morality has always been conceived as a personal and free response to the call of God, not a response to
an impersonal, detached law or precept. Although this in
itself would be a morality, the religious response is to Someone, to the saving God who by His initiative enters into a

relationship of creative and redeeming love of mankind. The value of the moral law, as St. Paul has pointed out insistently in the Epistles to the Romans and to the Galatians, is that it serves as a guide to this love. Its worth consists in that it determines love and acts as guide-post to the man who seeks to respond to God's initiative of love. By itself and in itself, considered apart from God, the law does not lead to a *religious* response but to morality, whereas the absolute norm of Christian morality is always the demands of a lived relationship of love with an absolute love. It cannot be stated too often that this must be appreciated existentially by the one who forms young religious.

No one, of course, denies the *theoretic* primacy of charity. What is required, however, is the lived awareness of this truth so that it permeates the atmosphere in which religious instruction is given and the firing of moral values takes place. St. Paul, out of his long experience of the struggle between law and love, repeats that the law of itself does not give the power to observe the law. It is a pedagogue which teaches man his need of Another, of the Saving God, if he is to express his love of God and fulfill the law. Man is not a slave to the law in the Christian dispensation but stands in an inter-personal dialogue of salvific love with God who made man and who intends to save him with his co-operation. The young religious, therefore, should be taught to be attached with his whole heart to the person of Christ who has entered human history to save him, but his efforts to express his loyalty to Christ by practical observance of the institute should never be allowed to deteriorate into that form of moralistic pharisaism which puts all the emphasis on the minutiae.

The moral teaching of St. Thomas Aquinas is wholly a

morality of dynamic orientation towards God as final beatitude. It is a morality of dialogue and not in any sense of pure legalism where the law is viewed as a limiting and final principle. That legalism which disguises itself under the mask of Christian virtue can create within young people psychological and spiritual difficulties which profoundly hinder normal religious evolution. Christian morality is always essentially positive in its orientation, and while certain things are prohibited, or expressed in negative form, what actually is forbidden is what impedes the full development of the life of charity. The prohibition has value only insofar as it facilitates our dialogual life with God and our neighbor, for virtues are positive and not negative dispositions. Virtue does not consist in the disposition to avoid something but in the choice of good which one achieves through the avoidance of negativity.[13]

There is a way of teaching positive law and positive obligations which by its very spirit seems to breathe a legalistic and formalistic atmosphere, as if the laws were objective procedures for sanctity completely independent of the Person towards whom they are orientated. Such preoccupation with the legalistic is frequently at the origin of psycho-pathological difficulties such as scruples, aggressivity and infantile rages. In his anxious search for an impossible perfection through the observance of every conceivable detail of law, the religious may run the risk of being thrown back into an unhealthy preoccupation with himself. At times an attitude which is legalistic in its essence is covered with a veneer of genuine spirituality, but this does not prevent the unconscious assimilations of attitudes fundamentally opposed to genuine Christian spirituality.

To appreciate vitally in a lived, existential fashion the

primacy of charity is not easy, since it calls for a profound exercise of faith and a transcendence of the entire natural realm of values. Formal values, legal values, ritual values can all too easily be substituted for divine values simply because we have a logical and ready inclination towards easily perceptible and easily codifiable realities. It appeals to man's inner insecurity if he can be hedged about by clearly grasped obligations, but the obligation which remains prime is: "Thou shalt love thy God and thy neighbor." The pharisaical preoccupation with the law as an independent final entity, the pharisaical concern with external behavior and with the minutiae and the accidentals of religious ritualism led in the time of Christ to that self-complacency and naturalism which He Himself vehemently condemned.

It is absolutely beyond any power of human nature to enter into that dialogue of grace which God has chosen to initiate with us. Of ourselves we are utterly powerless to begin our Christian life, and we should recall quite clearly that through the entire range of this religious life the initiative is always with God. Therefore, since grace itself transcends all the powers of our created nature we should not rely upon the immanent powers of nature to ensure fulfillment of law and duty.

Faith without works is an illusion, but it is also an illusion to believe that one can cultivate charity at the expense of the law. Nevertheless, the law itself remains subsidiary. Christ came to fulfill the law, for He was the Son of God, and incorporating us into Himself gives us the power to obey the law. The law is no longer a demoralizing principle pointing out our own weakness to us but a way of love, and it is an expression of that love for us. But beyond all law God asks a total adherence to Himself and to the community in charity. This charity should be a living source of the observance of all ritual, rules and precepts, for if these are observed without charity they are sterile and productive only of self-satisfaction. By ourselves we are unable to fulfill the demands of God completely, and this terrible inadequacy can be made up only by the living God who bends over us in a dialogue of love if we are willing to respond to Him. But if we put our sufficiency in ourselves we shall be left to ourselves. The absolute precept, the one absolutely normative principle of Christian life, is charity to God and man. Upon this all the law depends and by this it is fulfilled. Until he has grasped this fact, not only in its theoretic value but also in its existential implications, man can never attain maturity either in his psychological or in his spiritual life.

NOTES

1. E. O'Doherty, "Religion and Mental Health," in *Studies* (1956), pp. 39–49.
2. Dr. Suzy Rousset, "Quelques critères de maturité," in *Vie Spirituelle Supplément* (1958), p. 301.
3. *Ibid.*, p. 302.
4. D. R. Parrot and R. P. Romain, "Maturité affective et vie sacerdotale," in *Vie Spirituelle Supplément* (1958), p. 313.
5. Jean-Marie Le Blond, "Le Culte du Sacré Coeur et la psychologie moderne," in *Le Coeur du Christ*, ed. H. Rondet (Le Puy, Mappus, 1958), pp. 117–120.
6. M. Oraison, "Essai sur la peur dans la psychologie religieuse," in *Vie Spirituelle Supplément* (1952), p. 146.
7. Le Blond, *op. cit.*, p. 118.
8. *Ibid.*, pp. 122–125.
9. Rousset, *art. cit.*, p. 306.
10. Parrot and Romain, *art. cit.*, p. 308.

11. A. M. Henry, "The Mystery of Virginity," in *Chastity* (Newman, Westminster, 1955), pp. 86–87.
12. M. Oraison, *Fear or Constraint?* (New York, Kenedy, 1959), p. 127.
13. *Ibid.*, p. 125.

The Way of Poverty

4 The Way of Poverty

Poverty plays a central role in Christian thought, even as it was central in the life of our Lord. From the first moment of that life our divine Saviour made poverty the object of His love. He chose to be born of the poor, among the poor, in the poorest surroundings. He continually preached poverty by word and example, and He died poor and almost unattended on the cross. Indeed, He made poverty the first of the beatitudes, as though it held a peculiar attraction for Him, and in the Church, His continued Incarnation, we in turn make it the first of our religious vows.

The decisive importance of this great Christian virtue becomes apparent only when we realize that we are inserted into Christ's Body and are continuations of His Incarnate Self. For the Incarnation is everlasting, as St. Paul exclaims exultingly: "Jesus Christ, the Incarnate Word, yesterday, today and forever." Christ has come to our sinful race, a man with a human history, a man who had a certain nationality, a certain language and a certain human accent. He came, the longing of the prophets, "the desire of the everlasting hills," "the ancient of days," in our own nature to fashion for Himself a new humanity. God has become man that we might be deified. He has lifted up this human nature of ours to an unheard-of dignity. He has assumed a human nature for His own, so that He calls Himself by preference, and is, the very Son of Man. He has so exalted this sinful nature of ours that we truly adore the Sacred Humanity of God Incarnate. We offer the honor reserved to our very God to a human nature, the humanity of Jesus, united to the Eternal Word. Yet it was not for the sake of His own individual human nature that Christ thus dignified our manhood. It was not because He was needy that He took this humanity to Himself. He who is the "flashing forth of His Father's divinity, the express and perfect image of His Father's substance" knew no need. It was "for us and for our salvation" that He came. He came first and foremost to form for Himself a new race, a new humanity, which would be His Mystical Body—mystically, really, supernaturally united with Him. Members of this new humanity would be prolongations of His Incarnation, its extensions in time and space.

It is only when we realize fully the loving designs of Christ for all humanity and all creation that we are in the proper position to appreciate the profound significance of Christian poverty. It is true that without this understanding we can still realize the love Christ had for poverty. We need only see Him cradled in the manger to discover that preference. But because He wants Christians to prolong in themselves His thoughts and His judgments—"Let this mind be in you, which was also in Christ Jesus"—let us study further this central doctrine, in order that we may know more fully the Lord of poverty.

Because we are His members, it is evident that we should share the judgments of our head. We members should prolong in ourselves the appraisal of created goods characteristic of our master. Christ, the creator, never of course despised created things. All that God has made is good, and all this human universe of creatures has its own proper value and dignity. The poor man does not deny this but vigorously reaffirms it. Nevertheless, all this great universe has felt the effect of Adam's fall and it too, in the words of St. Paul, "groans for the day of its complete redemption," when as "a new earth and a new heaven" it will fully mirror the glory of God. Jesus has forever dignified our world in making it the home of His Incarnate Self, taking from it, from Mary's most pure body, His own. For He did not bring that body with him, as certain heretics have said, from heaven. Rather He lifted up to heaven the material body that the Virgin, the "Loom whereon was woven the garment of His flesh," prepared for Him. All earth and all earth's creatures received at that moment their vocation to a redemption that is as yet incomplete. We, His members, the mystical prolongations of His Incarnation, have the task of completing this redemption and of extending to all creatures the incarnational effects of the Word-made-flesh. All nature is, as St. Paul says, "in the pangs of childbirth" to bring forth this redeemed creaturedom. We, lowly and undependable humanity, are the divinely appointed midwives at this rebirth of nature. It is we who have the task of restoring to all creatures their proper dignity and role. It is we who bring all these creatures back to Christ. This is one of the fundamental meanings of Christian poverty. It is a reconsecration of the whole world of creatures to the Incarnate Word, their rightful head. It is we who consecrate them, dedicate them, order them anew to Him. We see this clearly in religious poverty, where nothing is used without having first been placed for disposal in the hands of the Incarnate Christ, through His Church, through our superior.[1]

If others have abused the world by too much use, we reconsecrate it by abstention, thereby achieving a great detachment from the world begun by the Incarnate Word and continued in us. For poverty is a spiritual destination imposed by us upon the creature in our very use, in our abstention, in our mere contemplation of it. "I will restore all things to Christ" is the saying of the poor man.

Poverty is above all a union with Christ, the master of the world, in whom the Christian wishes to possess everything, apart from whom he wishes for nothing. Poverty is the manifestation of a love that realizes the intention of love to give all, retaining nothing save hope. Poverty is a consecration of all things to Christ; an open affirmation before the eyes of the world that the world is well lost for Christ. Poverty gives to Christ the place He is destined to occupy at the center of the world. Poverty makes possible profound devotion to the mystical Christ still living among us. It is the poor who tend the poor and teach the poor and establish the Church in distant and missionary countries. There is but one Christ, and poverty frees us to love Him as He lives and breathes among us, neglected, forgotten, suffering, repeating in His mystical body the history of earth's treatment of Him in His life on earth.

In the Mystical Body, and in a special sense in religious communities, there is only one proprietor elected by our free decision—Christ the Lord.[2] No Christian has ever held that the possession of property is wrong. But it must be possessed with love and with freedom. It must be the thing possessed, and not that which possesses the owner. Even for the Christian, this ideal is not easy to attain. The existence in the Christian community of a poverty as total and free as religious poverty serves to recall to the world the possibility of freedom and the destiny of creatures. For poverty grants freedom to the soul, the freedom that we see in Christ the Lord, who moved in tranquil security to His destiny on the cross.

Poverty is freedom and also love. It gives the soul the capacity to understand and to appreciate the whole created world. Freed from self we may open our eyes on the world and behold the majesty of all that God has made. How well we see this freedom and contemplation in St. Francis, who having left all things, discovered all things anew. The soul that is poor is disengaged, ready for contemplation, for his eyes are opened. Poverty renders the soul more truly human, ready to behold the image of God who made it in all created reality. The Christian is neither blind nor indifferent to the universe, but finds in himself a secret sympathy for it, since in it he sees the invisible God and His Christ who has restored all things in Himself. The poor man of Christ is truly rich, for liberated from the dangerously constricting and narrowing influence of property, he finds himself mysteriously united to the God who has made all things. His is a sacrifice which unites itself to the sacrifice of Christ, who penetrates the whole of humanity and the whole of the universe.

When God created man He made him the center of the physical world and also the end of all things within that cosmos. Now, since the Incarnation, there exists another man, the Man Jesus, in His plenary humanity, to whom is ordered all the created world. The man vowed to poverty affirms this. He is like the explorer who has gone ahead and mapped out this difficult terrain of detachment, to reassure those who follow that such a journey is possible. He fulfills an important role in the Christian community, within which he creates a healthy atmosphere for Christian ownership.

The virtue of poverty, like every supernatural virtue, does expiation for the excessive attachment of Christendom to creatures. This expiation, begun by Christ in His life on earth, attains such plenitude that it overflows upon us, His prolongations. It implies a dependence that mortifies our perverse instinct for seeking security elsewhere than in Christ. It implies a dependence that excludes unconditioned ownership by referring all things first to Another. Before Our Lord and the Lord of the world, the poor man takes up a certain position as he renders back to Christ all that is naturally His. There is but one Christ, head and members, as St. Paul has so insistently taught us, and this same Christ repeats to the poor man today: "I was hungry and you gave me to eat; I was thirsty and you gave me to drink."

Let us never conceive Christian poverty as only one more ascetic means to union with God. It is much more than that if we regard it in the light of the Incarnation. It is an entering with Christ into the secret depths of His own redemptive work prolonged in us. It is an "engagement," a definitive commitment. It works towards the release of the whole world of bound-and-suffering-creaturedom that still sits in the shadow of darkness awaiting its full redemption.[3] The world in Christian theology is not a foreign prison-house in which the soul is chained for a period of trials. The whole world has been touched by the incarnation of the Son of God. No rock on the most distant mountain, no star, has remained unchanged by that event. The world has been, and always will be, the home of God's own Son, who reached into it for the matter of His body. Hence it is no "stranger-universe" to the Christian. It is simply a mute and longing universe that only we can free, repeating in ourselves the gestures of the Christ in our detachment and our preference of poverty. There is nothing in this world that does not require to be touched anew and humanized by being, in its own fashion, divinized. The echoes of this great news of our redemption are heard even in the material universe, and we, Christ's poor, are the instrument for transmitting these echoes of the great liberation.

The Christ who lives in this universe today, the Mystical Christ, still has need of this visible world, as He had in Galilee. Christ still asks for water from our springs and wells, as He did in Samaria. He still "has not whereon to lay His head," and if He is to find shelter and love, He will find it among the poor who have learned and who teach the destiny of creatures to all men. The poor are the ones to whom it is given to sing the hymn of the universe as Francis sang the "hymn to the Sun." The poor are the ones to whom Christ confides His Mystical Body in a special way, that it may not faint for want of the support of human members. The poor are the ones who affirm as real the humanity of the human Mystical Body of Christ as the early Fathers maintained against the heretics the reality of the human nature of the Physical Christ.

Christian poverty, then, has a profoundly Christian meaning. It is something quite distinct from the ascetic detachment of Buddhist monks. It is, and always will be, profoundly incarnational. We cannot forget in our practice of poverty this ultimate meaning and value. With our eyes

fixed upon "the author and finisher of our faith," we rejoice that He has given to us to share in His redemptive
work, that He has committed to our liberating care His
universe, and Himself, living on in His Mystical Body.

The eternal Son of God chose to become man, and in doing so, stripped Himself of the external honors due to His
humanity in its hypostatic union with the divinity. Thus,
in an essential sense, Christ is already poor from the very
moment that He becomes man under conditions of His own
choosing. His entire life was free from any sign of that
wealth or abundance which conduces to power in human
situations. His preference among human companions seems
definitely to have been for the poor. His mother and His
foster father were chosen from among them, and those
whom He picked to follow Him in the apostolic task were
poor men. Christ also pointed out that among the signs
of the arrival of the Messianic period was the fact that
the poor, who are generally ignored, had the good news
preached to them. "Blessed are the poor in spirit; the kingdom of heaven is theirs"; "See how the birds of the air never
sow, or reap, or gather grain into barns, and yet your
heavenly Father feeds them": His words have affirmation
in the words of St. John of the Cross: "Mine are the heavens
and mine is the earth." Christ promises to the poor in spirit
that they will possess all things in a spirit of detachment.

There is no doubt that Christ accepted help from various
people. He permitted the holy women to serve Him and
perhaps also to assist Him in taking care of the material
necessities of life, but those who surrounded Him were
ordinarily not marked by the pride of life or the power of
wealth. When the young rich man came to Christ, our Lord

looked upon Him with love and was willing to accept him among His companions, but He first underscored the lesson of detachment. This lesson has always been held in esteem in the Christian tradition.

Basically, esteem for poverty began without any theoretical basis other than imitation of Christ Himself. The early monks of the desert practiced it as an ascetical means to crush their pride and their attachment to this world and to give them the eschatological point of view. There is also closely connected with Christian poverty the ideal of humility. Generally speaking, in human affairs the man who possesses money possesses power and is consequently able to expect submission, adulation from those about him. He can purchase service and he can purchase flattery. It is a rare man of wealth in this world who is not touched by the pride which wealth brings with it. In the Christian tradition, however, a love for humility is closely allied to a love for poverty. The Christian understands not only that the practice of poverty brings a renunciation of every material thing not of absolute necessity, but that it preserves man, when it is lived in its true spirit, from temptations to vanity, pride, power and the urge for domination.[4]

Poverty is also closely allied with the virtue of hope. The poor man trusts in the providence of God and not in his own resources. For wealth generally brings with it natural security, making a man indifferent to that true security found in God alone. Yet we must always be ready to free ourselves from every natural ground of security and to cast ourselves wholly into the hands of God, our sole total good. The instinct for possession is so powerfully rooted in us precisely because the instinct of self-preservation and of self-sufficiency is deeply rooted in us. But the creature must always remember that while he needs a certain modicum of material goods to protect his life and those who are dependent on him, and a certain control of material resources to fulfill the possibilities of his personality, he does not live by bread alone. The great good of man is the possession of God, and the poor man is the man who makes public profession of the fact that his gaze is fixed on the good. He lives in a state directed towards the future. In whole-hearted abandonment to the eternal Father he takes up his position towards the dangers and difficulties of life, secure in the Father and not in the power of money. It is only God who can fulfill our desire for security and for love. The poor man realizes this, and makes a profession of it. Hence, in Christian tradition there has always been a mysticism of poverty. This does not mean, of course, that actual poverty is obligatory upon all or that vowed poverty is obligatory on all. Certainly poverty of spirit is an indispensable means for Christian fulfillment, but the religious who dedicates himself to poverty by vow is one who is drawn after Christ by inner understanding of humility and the cross.[5]

Obviously, every form of the religious life has its own characteristic poverty determined by the constitutions of the order or congregation. In today's apostolic life, poverty must always be considered in the light of the apostolate. There is nothing extraordinary in the communal possession of expensive equipment and material by religious. But those religious who use them must always cultivate an inner spirit of detachment in their use. They must use them "as though they used them not."

The religious makes a gift once and forever of all that

he possesses and of all that the future may give to him. In doing so, he frees himself, that he may follow a form of life closer to that of Christ and manifest his hope in the loving care of the eternal Father. It is possible that he will actually gain more in material comfort than he has lost, for one must admit that today many congregations of religious live in a state of material comfort and security surpassing in many details that of the ordinary people. Nevertheless, they live entirely dependent upon the will of another and upon the rules of their congregation; they possess nothing in private but all in common.

Even here, however, there is always the danger that just as a collective pride in the order may spring up in a certain organization whose members are individually humble with regard to themselves, so also, a congregation may at times come to look upon poverty in a way which ill befits a group professing religious values. In times past, as is well known, monasteries owned great tracts of land which enabled them to live in a style which can only be described as wealthy. Lay people are not scandalized by large houses, but they are shocked by anything which approaches vulgar ostentation and self-indulgence. Even though all the canonical requirements of the vow are observed in such a state, the spirit of evangelical poverty has lost its value as testimony to the Christian life. Hence there must always be evidenced in religious a genuine spirit of renunciation of material goods. A genuine distaste for superfluity must penetrate the use of even those things which are reserved in common. Otherwise the spirit which has sought freedom in its vows becomes ensnared in the luxury of shared possession.

When poverty is lived fully it genuinely frees the soul of man, humiliating him before God, making him receptive

to special graces. For in the necessity of continual dependence upon superiors in the use of all material goods the
poor man constantly opposes that innate selfish desire for
acquisition and security. The longing for pomp, pride and
power in life is effectively stilled by the continual recourse
to dependence.

It is quite possible, of course, for a soul which possesses
little in a quantitative fashion to be attached to this little
in a spirit of riches. Therefore the man who has vowed
poverty must check within himself the desire to find security
even in that small measure of material possessions which he
is granted. The vice of avarice can take root in the strangest
soil. There are those who are attached to their own collection of worthless trifles. The spiritual regard and attitude
of these religious towards their "collection," although the
content is of no material value, spontaneously call to mind
the miser. The Christian attitude should be that which
Christ urges us to cultivate: "Lay not up to yourselves treasures on earth where the rust and the moth consume and
where thieves break in and steal, but lay up to yourselves
treasures in heaven."

When the spirit of poverty has been lived for many years,
it gradually becomes part of the spiritual makeup of the religious, extending its domain from material possessions to all
possessions which may be an object of man's acquisitive faculties. Honors, reputation, influence, friendships, graces,
even spiritual gifts, are progressively brought under the domain of detachment, so that the Christian lives solely for
God. Detachment from one's own personal gifts—material,
natural and spiritual—comes to be part of the makeup of
the poor man, and his practice of poverty, which does not
change appreciably from the first moment to the last mo-

ment of his religious life in regard to material possessions, gradually becomes more interiorized.

Ultimately the final motive of poverty becomes the motive of theological hope. The poor man seeks God alone in the poverty of possessions, trusting to Him to open the avenue of approach to great possession. The soul which lives by poverty becomes a greathearted soul, after the image of Christ. The whole religious attitude of man becomes more humble, more reverent, more attendant upon the movement of God, more attentive and docile to the suggestions of God, more conscious of his deepest metaphysical need, his need for God.

NOTES

1. E. Mersch, *Morality and the Mystical Body* (New York, Kenedy, 1939), pp. 189–191.
2. E. Roche, "Le Mendiant de Dieu," in *Vie Spirituelle* (1954), p. 359.
3. Mersch, *op. cit.*, p. 187.
4. H. Graef, "La Vertu de Pauvreté," in *Vie Spirituelle Supplément* (1957), p. 130.
5. M. Labourdette, "The Theology of Religious Poverty," in *Poverty* (Newman, Westminster, 1954), pp. 116–117.

The Value of Virginity

5 The Value of Virginity

At a certain dramatic and unforgettable instant in the history of the human race the Word became flesh. The "unthinkable" became a reality; God became man. "Retaining His divine nature, the Son of God assumed a human nature" and made it indefectibly, eternally His. At this climactic point God entered time to make His own a human history and a human destiny. "For while all things were in quiet silence and the night was in the middle of her course, thy Almighty Word, O God, leapt down from heaven, from thy royal throne." At the moment of the Incarnation, God strode across the border of eternity and entered our temporal order. It was a decisive and purposeful act. The *Verbum*, the Word of God, deliberately assumed a human nature in a union so close as to surpass all our attempts to comprehend its intimacy. Some slight idea of how closely God united that human nature to Himself can be obtained from the realization that His divinity so penetrated the humanity that human nature may be said to exist within the divinity. So intimate is the union of that humanity with God

117

that we can contemplate this man of our race dying for us on Calvary and say with truth: "One of the Trinity is being crucified for us."

God entered humanity to take human citizenship. At that same moment He plunged His roots so deeply into our entire race, past, present and future, that no man can ever be free from its effects. Like a healing medicine He was poured into our open wounds, and by this beneficent contact He began to sanctify us—His race, His people, His family, His humanity. All men were thereupon called to realize a new destiny, for they were called to become literally members of Christ's body—not, indeed, of that physical body of Christ which once thirsted in Samaria, walked on Galilee's hills and died in Jerusalem, to rise and live again in heaven, but of His Mystical Body, the extension, the continuation, the mystical prolongation of His physical body on earth. The man who is part of this body, if he dies while yet living in it, will be saved, for we are redeemed as members of a body and not as isolated individuals. Christ has called all men without exception to enter into this union of His body. For He came to create a new race, the Christ-race, a new and "royal priesthood," to which all men should belong. It is the members of this priesthood, this new race, that we call Christians.

When God united Himself indissolubly to humanity He made of it a new humanity. Now we must all constitute one great man with Christ the head, and we the members; bound together by bonds so real that theologians describe them as physical. This was a revolution. All things were changed by this fact of the Incarnation; new virtues that man had never dreamt of shine in this unique figure of Christ. Who could really comprehend Christian charity if he did not know that Christ is God and Man? Who before Christ had ever plumbed the depths of meekness and humility? All things are renewed in this Incarnation, and it is only in view of it that man can understand Christian chastity or virginity.

The Jewish people, God's chosen ones, did not commonly cherish virginity. Joseph and Mary cherished it, for they were to live in the very atmosphere of virginity—in the care of the Incarnate God. But neither pagan nor Jew comprehended Christian virginity. One comprehends it only in the light that streams from the Incarnation.

Even the Christian understanding of virginity has undergone certain modifications in the course of the centuries. The meaning of virginity and its superiority to marriage has, to be sure, always been recognized, but there were periods when popular preaching sought to exalt virginity by depreciating the sacrament of matrimony. That is not, however, the attitude today. (Thus the initiator of the movement to renew the theology of marriage, Dietrich von Hildebrand, is also the one who has perhaps given us the most profound analysis of virginity itself.[1]) The time is now past when virginity would be opposed to marriage as the spirit to the flesh or as the soul to the body. Today virginity is related to the Incarnation and to the notion of spiritual marriage with Christ. Although this idea of virginity is not clearly explained in Sacred Scripture, the rite of the consecration of virgins applies to the virgin, man or woman, the scriptural theme of the Church as the Spouse of Christ. The ultimate meaning of virginity is thus seen in the light of the Incarnation itself.

In the Old Testament, in such Prophets as Osee or Ezechiel and in the Canticle of Canticles, the bond between Yahweh and His people is expressed in terms of the mutual love of marriage. Yahweh demands of His people a total fidelity and a separation from all other gods precisely because He has bound Himself to His people by marital love. Consequently, any infraction of the alliance between Yahweh and His people, any seeking after foreign gods, is called adultery. Nevertheless the Old Testament does not clearly stress the value of personal virginity. It is rather the race itself which is wedded to God; the individual virgin holds no important role in Old Testament theology. It is not until the moment when Christ appears among us—Emmanuel, "God with us"—and lives His virginal life that spiritual marriage with God is considered a norm for dedicated chastity and an explanation of it.

In Christ Himself human nature subsists entirely through its relationship to the divine nature. The human nature of Christ is a concrete, existent, individual nature which is wholly dominated by the divinity, wholly possessed by the divinity, wholly related to the divinity. All that is human in Christ is the humanity of God and of the Second Person of the Blessed Trinity because it is only He who has entered into our flesh. Although the entire Trinity creates the body assumed by Christ, it is nevertheless only Christ who becomes man, only God under the relationship of filiation who becomes incarnate. Thus the physical Christ is neither earthly Father nor earthly Spouse, because in all His earthly relationships He wishes to remain Son in the fullest sense of this word, always manifesting even in His humanity that filiation which is His proper perfection. If the earthly Christ is to be considered a Spouse, the espousals themselves must be understood as joining Him with the *whole* of humanity. He is the Spouse of the Church as well as its Head. In the purely individual sense of the word, however, Christ is neither earthly Father nor Spouse but virginal. He remains, as we have said, a Son of the Father in all His human relationships.[2]

In the light of this virginal life of Christ it is easier to understand the virginity of Mary. Christ the Redeemer has no need of a human father, and in a certain sense this shows how totally divine is the initiative of the Redemption. The virginity of Mary thus makes possible the marvellous union between herself and the Son of God, prefiguring the special union which the Church will consecrate under the term virginity, vowed chastity, for those who follow Mary in imitating this special relationship of hers to Christ. Finally, the virginal marriage of Christ and His Church is also symbolic of the state of consecrated virginity.

The New Testament thus has many overtones which the Old Testament lacked. In the Old Testament, as we have seen, Yahweh was described as espoused to the entire people of God. In the New Testament it is one of our own, a man, who enters into communion with humanity, and it is through this humanity of Christ that we continue to live in communion with the eternal Father. The Church is the Spouse of one who is both God and man. Just as Israel had to abstain from political alliance with foreign countries who worshipped false gods, so the Church in a sense transcends all nations; she is at once immanent to history and transcendent to it. Her relationship to God is conjugal, but a conjugal relationship valid not only for the whole body of the Church but for each member of this new race Christ has created. In the spiritual marriage which is the ultimate explanation of Christian virginity, the individual is handed over body and soul to the Lord.[3]

It is the perfection of our personal relationship to God resplendent in our very body and through the donation of our body which gives to virginity the fullness of its meaning. The virgin is literally constituted in a marital relationship to his or her Spouse, Christ.[4] Virginity thus arose in a Christian community more or less spontaneously as an expression of this total donation of a man in his body to the Christ human and divine. The body of the Christian belongs entirely to Christ. This is the normal Christian state of affairs. And yet, not every Christian is called to the life of consecrated virginity. Marriage is the total donation of heart, soul and body, one to another, in Christ Himself. It is Christ who is, so to speak, the erosphere in Christian marriage, it is He who holds the ultimate secrets of both personalities, and the ultimate themes of marriage can be realized in the fullest sense only in Him. The sacrament of marriage blesses the gift within Christianity of one body to another. As it is Christ Himself who guards the marriage bond in Christianity, so it is the same intimate bond between Christ and the Christian which founds both virginity and the sacramentality of marriage.

Both consecrated virginity and Christian marriage represent this close appurtenance to Christ, but in marriage, the husband and the wife represent for one another Christ and His Church, whereas in the state of consecrated virginity, the virgin refers himself directly to Christ without making use of a representative. Thus, the virgin confronts Christ face-to-face. The consecration ceremonies tell us that the virgin does not content herself or himself with that love which is implied in marriage, but that his or her love bears directly upon that which is symbolized and represented in marriage. Although the Church applies this specifically to women, the truth remains universal in the spiritual sense since all souls are feminine before God. The type of union of which we speak transcends human marriage and the division of the sexes.

As the sacrifice of the entire person to the Incarnate Christ, virginity is, as it were, the heart of the three vows commonly made in religion. Virginity represents a totally undivided heart, and as such explains Christian poverty, which prolongs this undivided heart into the *material universe* and which sacrifices all material goods for love to possess them again in the love of Christ. Obedience also manifests this virginal regard towards Christ with respect to *society*, because in religious obedience it is the Church who is the provident mother to the virgin. The exercise of virginity and poverty in a community requires obedience. This obedience is directed not merely towards the efficient division of the tasks of the institute but also towards making evident the virgin's undivided love for Christ. Thus through poverty and obedience the virgin prolongs in his social life and in his relationship to the material world that spirit of undivided donation to Christ.[5]

Virginity is essentially eschatological. Its central meaning of undivided appurtenance to Christ in marital relationship is directed primarily towards the end of time. Although marriage sanctifies the body and through it the entire material world in an incarnational universe, consecrated virginity is superior to marriage because it anticipates that final world of redeemed humanity which is now, in the words of St. Paul, groaning and waiting for its deliverance. When Christ speaks (Mt. 19:11–12) of those who have made themselves eunuchs for the kingdom of heaven He is speaking in

terms which directly recall the apocalyptic tradition of the
Old Testament. He is specifically evoking the fulfillment of
all history in the resurrection of the body when "the new
skies and the new earth" will be present as a hospitable home
to risen humanity. This fulfillment and that of the kingdom
of God will only take place when the sphere of human history has been closed with the resurrection of the body.

The virgin manifests this Christian fact: we are already
living in the last times, and we await the fulfillment of the
salvation of all human history, the resurrection of the body.
This does not imply that the virgin attempts to despise the
body or the corporeal universe. It simply indicates that he
or she anticipates the triumphant resurrection of the flesh
and bears witness to the faith of the Church in this resurrection.

We have not here a lasting city; the virgin makes that
evident. For virginity liberates the soul from certain obstacles, preoccupations, earthly ties which prevent us from fo-
cusing our attention upon the imminent return of Christ,
the Lord of history. St. Paul (in 1 Cor. 7:29, 31), indicates
that "the time is short," that "the figure of this world" is
already passing away. Human life, such as we know it on
this earth, under the conditions of this earth, is not destined
to endure forever.[6] The Christian must always keep this fact
before his mind. Consecrated virginity is thus an exterior
sign of the renouncement which is demanded of all in our
Christian life. It is a sign of our communal hope in the time
to come, the fulfillment of the kingdom.

It is characteristically Christian to be ever aware of the
imminence of Christ's coming. This is a religious truth and
the foundation of our Christian existence. Having already

died to sin and to the world (in the Johannine sense) at baptism, we are also already risen "in hope," and we already share with Christ the glory of His Father. We await the final revelation at the end of time when the resurrection of the body will complete our Christian lives. Already the germ of this divine life which will flower in heaven is in our souls, and it is neither numerically nor specifically different from that divine life which we will lead in heaven. Grace is the seed of glory, not merely its pledge.

At times it would seem that this eschatological meaning of virginity has been less in the foreground than it is at present, and yet it is always in the consciousness of the Church. The Christian who renounces marriage for consecrated virginity is always an indication of that waiting attitude which expects the Lord and the final establishment of the kingdom.[7] Virginity is an invitation to us to fasten our attention not upon the passing phases of this world but upon the world to come. Virginity reminds us that the Christian life must always strain towards a future term and can never so install itself in human history as to disregard the future of that history. By renouncing an essential element of human and earthly existence, virginity dedicates itself to waiting for the Lord and is like a second baptism. As, through his first baptism, the Christian is plunged into the death and resurrection of Christ, through the vow of virginity he dies to certain comforts of the human heart, to the dedication of himself in human love to another human personality and the prolongation of that love in its fruit and embodiment, the child. The virgin thus lives already the life of the resurrected flesh in an objective sense. At times in the ceremony of the vows of religious profession, a shroud is used to indicate that the virgin has now died to the fulfillment of human love in marriage, and this shroud is symbolic of burial with Christ that one may await with Him the triumphant resurrection.

Although the state of consecrated virginity is certainly superior to that of marriage, as the Council of Trent has declared, nevertheless, charity remains the heart of Christian perfection. The same faith, hope and charity animate both the virgin and the married Christian. However, the virgin by his or her state of life makes profession before the entire world of a marital relationship to Christ, thus recalling to the world its ultimate, supratemporal, supramundane destiny. Virginity takes its special form from the communion which it establishes between Christ and the individual soul. In the renunciation of one form of love, communion between two persons, the virgin establishes a new communion between himself and Christ. Again we see how virginity anticipates the end of temporal history, for it is evident that in the New Testament perfect union with Christ Incarnate is most intimately connected with the end of time. In fact, Christ our Lord constantly appeals to the symbolism of marriage to evoke the period of the end of time (John 2: 1–11; Mt. 22:1–14). He is continually represented as the spouse of the soul with particular reference to the end of temporal history. Thus it is that virginity assumes its full importance when it is explained in relationship to the world to come, for only then will be realized in its plenitude the marriage of humanity with Christ its God. Here on earth it anticipates this life under the sign of the cross with renouncement, sacrifice and in the light of faith. Marriage sanctifies all that is corporal and all that is material, and plunges man even to the very depths of his bodily life into

Christ, but virginity by-passes this form of the sanctification of earthly life to prefer the life of the world to come.

Marriage is a most profound form of earthly sanctification, and in the communion of charity and human love between the two persons even the most instinctive bodily reactions of man are sanctified. Because the marriage act evokes the highest possibility of which the body is capable, laying bare in its intensity and depth the very vital-corporal roots of the human personality, a most difficult and intense asceticism is needed to bring to holiness all the details of its activity. The soul must be actuated to as great a depth of intensity as is the body if the freedom and joy which are meant to accompany Christian marriage are to be experienced. The division which exists within the human personality because of concupiscence is profoundly felt in marriage, where human life is lived to its human completion and with the greatest intensity.

Virginity, on the other hand, transcends this division within the human personality. This does not mean that concupiscence is not present in the consecrated virgin, but because of the adoption of a way of life it is objectively transcended even though it may be subjectively experienced. Virginity as a state of life implies objectively a renouncement of the very sources of this division within the human personality, namely, the concupiscence of the flesh. Marriage, on the contrary, assumes and sanctifies human activity at the cost of a continual and progressive conquest of this division. In other words, what the married man or woman must gradually attain through the grace of God, the spiritualization of the flesh, the virgin accomplishes objectively and at once by his state of life.

Since virginity involves the sacrifice of one of the greatest means for purifying our egotism, the communion of persons in marriage, virginity becomes itself the sign of the objective manifestation of a deep personal communion, an I-to-Thou communion, of the Christian with Christ Himself. It refuses one form of charity only to assume a higher or total form directed immediately to Christ Himself. Virginity thus represents the state of the Christian soul in the risen life where the immediate presence of the Triune God is experienced, filling the soul of the Christian with a bridal joy in the presence of its spouse.

Virginity has also an ascetical significance inasmuch as it involves a renunciation of the goods of the body and of a domain in which the tendency to concupiscence is especially strong. Even when there is question of legitimate satisfactions, there remains in fallen human nature the danger of yielding to pride and concupiscence; even when man legitimately seeks pleasure he is allowing his elementary instincts a certain freedom of outlet which can all too easily become contaminated by excess. Asceticism demands that in order to strengthen our control over instinctual life we renounce at times goods which in themselves are perfectly lawful, such as the satisfaction gained from work or innocent pleasure. The spiritual person thereby emerges from the weakness of his natural position with regard to the things that please the senses and attains a higher control over the body, its instincts and pride.

In one sense such asceticism is a prudent measure designed to train the will to strength in time of temptation; in another, it is a prudent avoidance of every occasion that might involve even the danger of deliberate venial sin. Then again it may express a form of detachment from the goods of this world and a longing for the freedom of the children of God.

Virginity is a road to holiness inasmuch as it constitutes a union with God through the renunciation of the goods of the flesh. Viewed as an ascetical means virginity is a purification through self-denial very much like that of mortification, obedience or poverty. It is a *condition* which the ascetic assumes for a more perfect union with his beloved. In this sense, virginity is a strong determination to live for Christ alone and to renounce every other good rather than risk separation from Him through imperfection in the sphere of bodily pleasure. Thus virginity lays the foundation for a more profound union with Christ and is an effective means for surmounting certain obstacles to that union.[8]

Virginity also frees the heart from the occupation of earthly ties, so that the ascetic can give himself more completely to God. This means that the ascetic first of all realizes the lofty and noble nature of Christian marriage but is nevertheless willing to detach his heart from another created individual in order that he may love God more exclusively. The motive is undivided allegiance to Christ. The danger of a divided heart is obviously very great where there is question of human love. For the greater the good loved the more it tends to take possession of the loving person, and in the case of another human being whom we love with body and soul there is always danger that our love may be divided between God and this person. Virginity, by renouncing that communion of love and of the whole stream of life which Christian marriage represents, attempts to preserve man's heart completely for Christ.

There is always the danger, of course, that some inferior earthly good may try to fill the void left by renunciation of

marital love. The man who is married and who has dedicated himself to Christian love has broken down one of the
great forces of egotism, has destroyed within himself the
hard insensitivity characteristic of the bachelor. But it is all
too easy for the virgin to compensate for lack of earthly
love with ill-disguised affective and emotional entangle-
ments of the natural order, such as particular friendships,
or with other natural goods valid in themselves. For example, in place of natural love one can substitute a desire for
honor or for power. One can substitute a natural pleasure in
one's own talent and its fulfillment. One can seek a superficial life of excitement, entertainment and social activity.
For the virgin to fulfill his vocation he must constantly re-
mind himself that virginity evacuates a great human good
from his life precisely to fill that life with the divine love for
Jesus and not in order to leave him free to indulge his longing for power, for creativity, for natural human success or
for superficial diversions.

Virginity is a dangerous state. It is a supernatural state.
It should not be entered into lightly. The one who dedicates
himself by a vow to God should be aware that he stands in
an objective face-to-face relationship to Jesus, the most
beautiful among the sons of men, and that he cannot with
impunity substitute any idol for Christ. This is why Christian tradition constantly stresses that the consecrated virgin
becomes such only at the express invitation of Jesus, the
Spouse, who grants to the soul the graces needed for the renunciation of the great human good of marriage and the
power to live according to this difficult state of life.

Virginity is without meaning if it does not denote an affective state and a marital consecration to a Person in the

intimacy of personal love. It is love alone that gives virginity its adequate explanation and its reason for existence —love of the Incarnate Word and love of all those who are His mystical continuation upon earth. Virginity is an attitude of soul that Christ has inspired in His followers, and its ultimate explanation is found in Him. The virgin offers to Christ an undivided heart, one that is occupied with the unique object of his love: Christ the Lord. St. Augustine puts it well: "The joy of Christ's Virgins is Christ Himself; their joy is in Christ and after Christ, it is by Christ and for Christ." The virgin has one preoccupation: "The Incarnate Christ." But even so, this undivided heart does not reveal the total glory and dignity of Christian virginity. Virginity has a still deeper and rarer significance.

The virgin proclaims to all the world the supreme loveableness of this Person, Jesus, for whose sake he has forsaken all things. The world in turn, beholding the virgin, recalls that all things are well forsaken for the love of Christ the Lord. In the Christian community the virgin reminds the married Christian of his high dignity and vocation, of his high call and difficult mission. For the virgin provides that atmosphere of freedom and of all-conquering purity, that atmosphere of joyous spiritualization of the flesh, without which Christian marriage cannot be what it is called to be. The virgin thus is the guardian, by the example of his life, of the purity of marriage itself. But even this splendid care for Christ's Mystical Body is not the ultimate ground for Christian virginity.

The virgin, teaching the Christian community that we have no lasting city, by his vocation already anticipating the life of heaven, proclaims the redemption of the flesh, and proves by his triumphant transcendence over it the very divinity of the Christ who empowers him for this angelic life. The virgin is the living proof in the eyes of the world of the divinity of Christ's Church, in whom he lives, and by whom he lives. He embodies in a concrete way the eternal truth that "one thing is necessary," showing forth a visible and tangible preference of God above all His creatures; he objectifies what all Christians know: that "the Lord is above all His creatures." And yet all these splendors of Christian virginity still do not give us its ultimate meaning, so deep and so glorious is that meaning.

"The ultimate and the fullest meaning of virginity is simply this: This Christian virgin, man or woman, is the bride of Christ. Decisively, irrevocably, objectively, entirely, the virgin, man or woman, places the secret of his or her own personal mystery in the hands of Jesus and opens the heart to Jesus in a surrender that exceeds in intimacy and depth the surrender of marriage. The virgin is mystically married to Jesus. . . . This supreme self-surrender of the entire person to Jesus, radical, complete, for all of life, means that the virgin in a unique sense lives for Jesus, and for Him alone. . . . The whole center of gravity of the Christian virgin has been changed from earth to heaven; he already lives, as it were, the life of eternity."[9]

Not that the virgin ceases to live by faith and attains to vision. On the contrary, he lives very much by faith; but the personal relationship which the virgin assumes to Christ by vow is a relationship of such intimacy that it can only be described in terms of the confrontation of two souls in love. By this decision to reserve from all men the personal mystery of himself and open its deepest strata only to Jesus, the virgin becomes, as it were, wedded to Jesus, united to Him in an objective intimacy that is quite independent of feelings or sentiments. No matter what his feelings may be, the virgin soul is established in an intimacy with Jesus which spiritualizes his whole being, and lends it already a hint of that radiance which the glorified body will display in heaven.

Yet the virgin, united with Christ in this mysterious intimate relationship, does not take from Christ's members the love he gives to Him. That would be a small compliment to Christ become Incarnate for us. On the contrary, virginity is the condition for a more universal and more selfless love, a love that sees primarily the soul of all men and does not seek itself in any form. Consecrated chastity has this widening and humanizing influence, and if it does not succeed in liberating the virgin's heart, if it leaves him selfish, dry and hard, withdrawn, and capable only of a cold substitute for authentic love, then it has not reached its plenitude. For in its fullness virginity is always the condition of a more perfect and more dedicated love of Christ's members. Indeed the martyrs who have died for this extension of Christ's incarnation have most often been virgins, and the "white" martyrs who have lived for it on earth, teachers, nurses, missionaries, sisters in orphanages, asylums, and homes for the aged, priests and brothers in prison camps—those who have made his name honored even by the unbeliever—these, the great lovers of mankind, have most often been virgins.

This is the atmosphere of chastity and virginity that we absorb in the company of Jesus. He teaches us how to be divinely human, in imitation of Himself. All love is naturally and normally fertile; we must not forget that virginity too is fertile, and even doubly so. Because of this love that is chastity, the poor will have always their servants, the child

will have always a mother, and the great mass of humanity,
Christian and pagan, will have always before Jesus an intercessor whose austerities, vigils, suffering and weariness
speak for him. Finally, the spouse of Christ is an intercessor
whose bridal relationship to Jesus and whose bridal love of
Jesus offer splendid hope that His mercy will be abundant
for all miserable and sinful humanity.

NOTES

1. *In Defense of Purity* (New York, Sheed and Ward, 1933), pp.
   183–196.
2. Mersch, *Morality and the Mystical Body*, p. 231.
3. A. M. Henry, "Le Mystère de l'homme et de la femme," in *Vie
   Spirituelle* (1949).
4. Hildebrand, *op. cit.*, p. 184.
5. J. M. Perrin, *La Virginité* (Paris, Ed. du Cerf, 1952), p. 77.
6. Msgr. Paulot, "La Virginité Chrétienne," in *Vie Spirituelle*
   (1958), p. 411. Cf. "Le Sens de la virginité," in *Christus* (January, 1958), pp. 33–36.
7. Divo Barsatti, "La Virginité," in *Vie Spirituelle* (1953), pp.
   148–149.
8. Hildebrand, *op. cit.*, pp. 150–156.
9. *Ibid.*, p. 188. Cf. Ch. Héris, "L'Amour Virginal," in *Vie Spirituelle*
   (1951), pp. 68–69.

The Notion of Obedience

6 *The Notion of Obedience*

If the Christian searches the depths of his personality, he finds that his nature is given him by another, Christ, who possesses him. If he searches the depths of his will activity, he should find there the same Christ. This is one meaning of Christian obedience and the vow of obedience: as the source of our Christian existence is Christ, so the ultimate source of all our willing should be in Him if it is to be Christian willing.[1]

By establishing a Church, with a head and authority to command, Christ sets us on our way towards prolonging His will. For the Church has authority to command and to approve, and the Church has approved the institute in which the religious obeys. The authority of the Church is derived from Christ, whose continued Incarnation she is. This authority she confers, in a measure regulated by law and by the particular institute, on the religious superior. In a strictly juridical sense, therefore, it is true to say that he who obeys the religious superior obeys the voice and authority of Christ, who lends authority to the superior that he

137

may build up the body of Christ. Not that Christ has promised to the religious superior the gift of infallibility; He has promised, however, that the subject in obeying is infallibly doing the will of God.

This is not to say that were Christ physically present He would have commanded precisely that which the superior commanded. Christ's wisdom is divine, whereas that of the superior, even granting the grace of state and guidance by the Holy Spirit, remains limited and fallible. What we do mean, however, is that since Christ chose to have a human body and to be prolonged in His Church by human members of that body, He ratifies the decision of the superior. With His all-encompassing wisdom He knows how to draw out the best from the act of obedience, a thing impossible to the subject even though his decision were, humanly speaking, better than that of his religious superior.

If what the superior commands is humanly speaking imprudent, Infinite Wisdom engages itself to remedy the defect. It does not engage Itself to assist the disobedient subject even though he is disobeying an imprudent command. Since this delicate task of representing Christ has been committed to the superior by the Church, His prolongation, it is clear that the superior should try to do just that—represent Christ in the wisdom, kindness and love that He manifests in His decisions. He commands with love and His commands are received with love—this is the normal state of obedience. Between the loving superior and the loving subject there arises by faith the vision of Christ. In His name one commands and in His name one obeys; He commands them both, and each in the other venerates the loving Christ.

By obedience the subject substitutes for his private judgments and decisions the judgments and decisions of the Incarnate Word prolonging Himself both in the superior and in the subject. Thus obedience is above all a union of will with Christ, so that all our actions and decisions are the activity of Him in whom we live and move and have our being. As the branch lives by the vine, so we live by our insertion into Christ our head, who in obedience communicates His mind and will by prolonging His decisions in us. It is in this way that Christ preserves our wills from their native instability, and rescues them from error and aberration.

We see, then, how obedience is an affirmation of our faith in the Incarnation. No one who denies the reality of Christ's Mystical Body can possibly comprehend the nature of obedience as it is practiced in the Church. No one who thinks that the Incarnation is an event in the distant past without prolongation in the present can comprehend the inner meaning of obedience. Obedience is a gracious affirmation before all the world of the reality, the dignity and the wisdom of the Incarnation of the Son of God.

Since obedience is an insertion of our will into the will of our Lord still operative upon earth, still active in building up for Himself the fullness of His Mystical Body, it is always and essentially unitive. Obedience unites us to the will of the Incarnate Christ and to His work. God's energy is dedicated to the building up of this Mystical Body, and it is precisely to this work that He unites us.[2] In fact, He lets the obedient subject share His plans, His decisions, His procedures in this "divinest of all works," the redemption of the world. Obedience is thus a great homage to the Incarnation. Christ lowered Himself to take on human nature for us and for our salvation. We in turn adore this God made man in His Incarnation and are willing to extend our reverence to

His extension in time and space, and to the superiors who, through the will of the Church, function in the Church, His Mystical Body.

Obedience is a virtue that operates quasi-sacramentally. It gives grace to the subject through the instrumentality of the material human being who is the superior, as the sacraments give grace through matter because of the fact of the Incarnation of God. For as the sacraments are the gestures of Christ morally prolonged in time and space, so the human voice of the superior is the prolongation of the plan of the Incarnation. He who hears this voice hears the voice of God, for God planned it so when He accepted the instrumentality of matter and a body in His Incarnation. Having made His material body an instrument of grace, He now makes the voice of the superior an occasion for grace. We might profitably ask ourselves how strong is our belief in the Incarnation, how ardent is our belief that this material body of Christ is literally the Body of God, how firm is our faith in the truth that the material body which He carried to crucifixion and to death was anointed with the divinity itself? And we might well examine how basic is our affirmation of God's *wisdom* in using lowly matter as the instrument of the divinity. Our whole incarnational concept of the world is implicated in the virtue of obedience, which makes us love the orders of a human superior because he holds a particular place in this Mystical Body of Christ.

"I am come that they may have life," our Lord has declared to us, "and may have it more abundantly" (John 10: 10). This is the text that gives us the secret of obedience. He has come to elevate our life, our activity and our decisions, uniting them with His decisions and redemptive activity. That our wills may take part in this redemptive activity, that they may be themselves redeemed from selfishness and error, God has created this state of obedience to unite our acts to His. With Him and in Him, we build up, with God the Father, the Body of Christ. Obedience is our way of growth. It is not a shrinking of our true selves but a development, for we become more fully human by becoming identified in will with the Humanity of Christ. We set our wills to the tasks of Christ for the love of Christ that they may be perfected by sharing in the power, love, initiative and activity of the will of Christ the Lord.

Obedience itself, like most other Christian virtues, has its caricatures. Just as the legitimate desire for mystical union with God deteriorated at various periods into illuminism, just as a mystique of poverty in the Church created a false accent on poverty, so too obedience has known certain dangers. There is, in fact, a false mystique of obedience. This may sound strange to the person accustomed to being told that he must obey as a corpse or as a staff in an old man's hands. These and similar expressions suggest that it is impossible to obey too well. Obedience has traditionally been accepted as the sign of the soul docile to the suggestions of the Holy Spirit, for such souls are willing to submit themselves to legitimately constituted authority. Is it possible, then, that there can be exaggeration in the matter of obedience? Doubtless we have all heard the stories of St. Theresa and St. Margaret Mary obeying their human directors at the cost of inner anguish, and sometimes, apparently, even at the cost of conflict with illuminations received in prayer.

We must keep in mind that modern civilization is undergoing a period of crisis, accompanied by the re-evaluation of traditional values. The bewilderment in our society has inevitably made itself felt in the sphere of personal responsibility. On the one hand, this is manifested in the distrust of authority by modern youth which we have described. But on the other hand there is the danger that the bewildered Christian will resolve his conflict by placing too great confidence in submission to authority. Thus a false mystique of obedience can be created, for the interior spiritual activity of man can never be substituted for by a series of orders. To attempt to replace by an extrinsic directive power extending to every detail a profound inner action of intelligence and will is to attempt a dehumanization of man completely contrary to the spirit of obedience.[3]

Inevitably the Christian is to some extent molded by the society of which he is a part, and the twentieth century has tended to stress widespread ideologies which consider man as attaining his ideal when he obeys orders irrespective of their content. Communism, Nazism, all forms of totalitarianism attempt to create an intellectual and moral culture within the individual by way of orders from outside him. This attempt to fill from the outside the entire spiritual content of consciousness, to dragoon all inner volitional and intellectual movements so that man may become more docile, admittedly makes for order, but it does not necessarily make for spiritual development. If the nineteenth century rendered a sort of idolatry to the great teacher, revering anyone who could illuminate the intelligence, the twentieth century has clearly gone in another direction: the commander has been substituted for the teacher. And the intention of the ruler is not to illuminate the subject but simply to dominate and coerce his will. This poses a major threat to the intellectual and spiritual life of the subject.

One must always remember that the theological virtues— and particularly the highest of them, charity—should be the object of man's special cultivation. The purpose of a human being is to love God above all things, and obedience has the role of assisting and directing this development and fulfillment of the moral and theological virtues. It is not a substitute for inner action and should not be conceived as such. A pseudo-religion of the superior, a mystique in which one would immolate all one's individual and personal life to his action, would be very dangerous. Human leaders, even human superiors in religious life, ordinarily reveal their natural fragility sooner or later. It is particularly dangerous if the young subject has made such a human leader the center of his life. If one has elevated a superior to the center of one's spirituality where he is encompassed by faith, hope and love, one may have prepared the way for a subsequent collapse should the human leader himself collapse.

It is particularly true of immature religious that they sometimes assign to obedience a role which is not actually assigned to it in Christianity. At times they seem to make obedience the final end, as though it were the unique value in the spiritual order. At no period of life, however, may one abdicate personal freedom in order to be certain of not disobeying God. This is not the will of God for our human or our supernatural development. One does not enter into religious life to do the will of one's superior but to fulfill one's divinely given talents in the order of nature and grace, to practice the theological virtues, and to adhere to God. It is not the human directives of the superior that are the ultimate source of one's activity but the will of God communicated to one through the legitimately established institute. There is a certain temptation discernible at times in religious persons to translate all interior acts, even those of the theological virtues spontaneously suggested to them by the Holy Spirit, into acts of obedience. No doubt these religious are very well-intentioned, but there is an error at the base of such spirituality.[4]

St. Thomas Aquinas points out to us that obedience ranks below the theological virtues inasmuch as it is part of the moral virtue of justice. It is subordinated to the theological virtues, which directly and immediately put the soul in contact with God, and is in no sense a substitute for these virtues.

It is perfectly normal that the life of grace develop itself without continual recourse to outside directives. It is a universal law of organic beings that life must not be substituted for by exterior mechanisms, and that attempts to do this usually end in disaster. In its education the intelligent soul must be led to accept and to see for itself certain ideas and ideals. The same is true of the spiritual life, and a superior or director should not attempt to substitute himself for the activity of the Holy Spirit. It is not the ideal of religious obedience to construct a machine "capable of anything."[5]

Christians have, as their leader and chief, Christ who is also God. We glory in Him precisely because His command is identical with eternal, subsistent truth. We obey Christ without reserve because in obeying Him we obey truth itself. It would be folly, therefore, to base our theory of obedience on the prestige of any particular superior or upon the supposedly intrinsic value of exterior orders over the interior suggestions of the Holy Spirit. Obedience has a great role to play in Christian life, but this obedience always involves a free inner acceptation by the subject of the will of his superior. The subject does not substitute the will of his superior as an extrinsic thing for the free intelligent activity of his consciousness, but accepts the will of the superior and freely makes it his own so that he understands and fulfills it with intelligence and love. Obedience such as this leads to and supports the exercise of divine charity, but it is essentially a free, intrinsic attitude on the part of the subject, not a blind abnegation of all personal life and responsibility. Such an abnegation could never be approved by God.

The superior functions as the administrator of an objectively approved institute within the Church. His commands are channeled within the framework of this particular institute, which, judged by all norms of human and divine prudence, will lead the subject and the superior to sanctity. Religious obedience, then, is not primarily an obedience to the will of another but to an objective set of laws, precepts, and counsels, which the divinely guided Church has declared with certitude are a secure path to holiness. Obviously, the superior is never to be obeyed if he commands anything contrary to the law of God. The subject can never abdicate his responsibility before God to the extent that he simply obeys a human person, however legitimately constituted, rather than the law of God Himself.

On the other hand, it is difficult to explain in what sense the decisions of the superior are the decisions of God and the superior is the interpreter of the divine will. It is difficult because we cannot say simply that what the superior wills in a given case God Himself would have willed had He been functioning as the human superior in that situation. We cannot say this because, as we have already pointed out, God himself has never assumed the obligation to direct religious superiors immediately and infallibly in every decision. Nor

has He given superiors any charism or gift of the Holy Spirit
by which they may determine with certitude the divine will
in concrete situations. The superior must use the same human means to determine the divine will that the subject
himself must use. He has, it is true, special graces given him
by God in virtue of the special task which is committed to
him. He has also, generally speaking, a far more complete
grasp of the situation than has the subject, since he is in a
position to know details which the subject usually cannot
know. He is, ideally, in contact with the concrete situation
through the channeled initiative of all parties engaged in it.
Nevertheless it is obvious that all kinds of human factors can
have their effects on his decisions.

The command of the superior may arise from laziness and
a desire to follow the path which in the past has proved correct if not particularly fruitful. It may arise from human
limitations of intelligence or even from moral defects. Normally speaking, superiors are not conducted to sanctity by
any path other than that open to the subject. Consequently,
the subject cannot throw off all personal responsibility and
obey without question, when his intelligence points out to
him that problems, difficulties, dangers—perhaps serious
ones—to the community life or to the apostolate are in-
volved. There is no virtue in simply substituting another's
will for God-given personal responsibility.[6]

In certain situations, then, where the subject sincerely
and humbly believes he is in the possession of knowledge
which is not available to the superior, he must in conscience
inform him in order that he may make his decisions in the
light of such knowledge. It is possible that in some cases the
subject must go beyond the immediate superior and take

the matter to a higher authority. At times this is not done when it should be done because the subject yields to cowardice, fear of reprisals, disengagement, passivity. There is no doubt that a subject can, though with uneasy conscience, dispense himself from appealing to higher authority through fear of unpleasantness. Nevertheless, the subject may not excuse himself from pointing out to the superior dangers in a particular path of action, especially where the apostolate is in question. If the superior gives a command which is irrational, it is clearly not virtuous to obey without first attempting to understand it, to see its inner rationality. If, after prayerful examination, the subject is convinced that he has just and valid reasons for believing the command irrational and destructive to the good of the community, or to the work engaged in by the community, he must then take the matter to higher superiors.

This is a situation which is perhaps likely to occur more frequently in the complexity of modern religious life than in the simpler forms of monastic life. The religious superior today, at the head of an institution engaged in highly specialized work, is most unlikely to be a specialist in all the fields in which his subjects labor. It is quite possible that he will make an error in judgment, and sometimes one which is little short of disastrous. In such a case the subject may not calmly abdicate all responsibility to the superior as if he himself had no loving concern for his institute, his community or the apostolate in which his community is engaged. On the contrary, even anticipating the unpleasant reaction which the superior may possibly have, he must call his attention to the factors in the situation which he believes the superior has overlooked. And when it is a serious affair, and not simply a detail of religious life, he must also take the matter to higher superiors so that he may accept their judgment in peace and conscience.[7]

Religious obedience will always be a cross because the individual egotism of the subject will be constantly chafed by the necessity for molding his judgments, decisions and actions according to the judgments, decisions and will of another. But unnecessary crosses should not be added by the superior. Neither is he to govern by whim, personal prejudice, or by the interest of a social or age group to which he may happen to belong.

Both subject and superior have distinct obligations in religious life. Religious obedience is not a form of totalitarianism, and the superior himself retains moral responsibility for his decisions. He is not an autonomous source of control over other people's existence, and there would be grave danger if religious authority were to deteriorate to a lust for power. We must, however, face the fact that the urge to power is fundamental in human life, at least as fundamental as the sex urge. Ascetical advisors throughout the centuries have warned religious to beware of those forms of activity which could lead to temptations against chastity. It is just as necessary to point out to those who by the will of God have been constituted in power over other people's lives that certain temptations may accompany that situation. Thus, for instance, the temptation to disregard the opinion of others normally becomes greater as one continues in a position of authority. There can be no doubt that after a certain length of time all human authority tends automatically to identify the interests of the institution and the monastery with its own interests, prejudices and opinions.

Another temptation arises from the fact that subjects are reluctant to call their superior's attention to errors in judgment which they may have made. This reluctance is intensified when experience has forced subjects to admit that the superior is not interested in opinions differing from his own, although he may make use of the formality of asking for them. The religious superior must always try to make himself adaptable and open to suggestions, lest he find himself with an entourage whose "yea" is a secret "nay."

This is no small temptation, since in the highly concentrated form of living that the religious life is, a subject does not easily find the humility to return more than once with suggestions if the first ones have been rejected out of hand. It is an astonishing fact that a superior can be totally unaware of the convictions of his community on a point of procedure even where disapproval may be universal. The superior in that case normally has himself to blame. His previous conduct has usually brought it about that the members of his community no longer have the courage to fulfill their responsibility to use their God-given initiative to help the superior in the governing of the order.[8]

But if superiors have distinct temptations to meet and overcome in their exercise of authority, subjects also have to convert themselves to a proper appreciation of their vocation to obedience.

Today, as we have seen, the whole structure of religious life is often under attack because of those who say that they cannot abdicate their personal responsibility in favor of any other merely fallible human being. This error fails to take into account the fact that the fallible human being who is the superior is juridically constituted by the Church to administer the institute which the Church has approved as a way of sanctity.

The very stuff of which Christian life is made is obedience. Christ announced that His will was to do the will of the Father. In like manner the Christian has given himself to Christ, intending to do the will of the Father indicated to him by divine law. In this sense, the law has the function of a divine pedagogue instructing the Christian on the path to liberty. God first gave to the Jews minute prescriptions for educating their attitudes towards Himself. It was the law itself which was to conduct them to the Christ. The truth is still in effect today: the Christian begins life with the liberty of the children of God because he is baptized into that freedom. But still the law of sin, of concupiscence, remains within him and is ever active. Man remains carnal, sold over into sin, and he does not accomplish the good that he wills but rather, as St. Paul tells us, "the evil that he wills not." This is where the law enters in and brings him to the adult age of Christ. Obedience acts as a teacher which, through a long and patient process in education, conducts the Christian towards the perfect liberty of the children of God. Instead of a life devoted to all the chance desires and caprices of his personality, the obedient Christian follows a law laid down to him by Incarnate Wisdom. Instead of being dominated completely by the reactions of his affective life and following the impulses of self-love, the Christian submits himself patiently to the law that he may learn to follow what is his objective good, the will of God. Obedience is thus the school of charity and of freedom. It puts man on the road towards renouncing his own will and humbly learning to accept in its place the will of God. Thus man joins himself completely with the divine will and renders to God that total homage of himself and of all that he possesses of which St. Thomas speaks (2, 2, a. 186, a. 51).

St. Thomas states, in fact, that the obedient man should preserve a spontaneity and joy in following the will of his superior. This is possible psychologically if we remember the statement of Thérèse of Lisieux: "I do always my own will because I have made the will of my superior my own." However, even at the highest point of religious perfection, although the religious has less need of distinct exterior direction, he still has need of obedience to the interior suggestions of the Holy Spirit.

It is the will of Christ to unite all men to Himself and, through Him, with the Father. Consequently, the new humanity will accept the will of Christ and the will of God as the will of their Father. The very first disposition of the Christian vocation is thus to lay oneself open to the action of God. Man is primarily receptive, and not creative. The kingdom of God is not so much established through our efforts as it is received as a gift from on high. What God seeks in order to create sanctity is material that is receptive, that is willing to receive His divine impressions. All through His life Christ manifested extraordinary devotion to the will of the Father. He accepted the conditions of human life completely, putting aside only that which could not stand with His sanctity or mission. He lived the human life with a full heart. He knew fatigue, He knew exhaustion, He knew rejection and failure, but He accepted them all as the conditions of human life. In His work He uses time, good and bad weather, all the ordinary material of human life, because He responds to the Father with a complete acceptation of the Father's will.

The temptation to the extraordinary way does not move

Christ, nor should it move the Christian. The normal routine of life and submission to the laws of God are the Christian's road to sanctity. St. Thomas Aquinas points out that "obedience is a virtue which places man correctly in the universe, assigns to him his proper rank in the play of secondary causes." It is obedience to the law which permits man to participate in that vast "cosmic liturgy." By submitting himself to the law of God and to his human superiors, man submits his freedom voluntarily to the order which God Himself has established, and thus he sets himself in truth and grows in charity.

This same educative force of obedience is evident in religious obedience. The obedience of the religious educates his liberty, freeing him, as we have said, from the caprices and deceptions to which all men are subject. The Christian receives at baptism not a spirit of slavery but a spirit of adoption, and he prizes his liberty rightly. Perhaps no century has so prized liberty as our own. But today there are often grave crises of vocation simply because of the inability to solve the apparent conflict between liberty and religious obedience. As we have observed in earlier contexts in this book, the man of today is unwilling to surrender his liberty and his independence unless he is certain that he is giving up these values for greater personal values. If religious obedience is presented to him as an immolation of freedom, he will reject it. If obedience seems to the Christian to involve a mutilation of his personality, then it is not likely that he will be attracted to it.[9]

In the past superiors sometimes thought to train their subjects in a very peculiar fashion. A neat set of gymnastic exercises was constructed to "break the will," and stupid and irrational commands were given. The defense for such a procedure was sometimes the authority of the Fathers of the desert, whose apostolate was, after all, somewhat different from that of our times. Today, as we have noted earlier, such practices are both obsolete and repulsive.[10]

Christian obedience, and particularly religious obedience, has as its purpose the development of the adult Christian. Jesus Himself has preached for His disciples a sovereign liberty with regard to the prescriptions of the Mosaic Law, and St. Paul has certainly exalted this whole notion of Christian liberty in comparison with slavery to the law. In his continual conflicts with the Mosaic mentality, Christ Himself has given us a magnificent lesson on the importance of liberty in the Christian life. St. Paul celebrates the death of the Mosaic law as Mosaic, and rejoices that the spirit of Christ has made us free in Christ Jesus (Rom. 7:6; 8:2). If Christ has liberated us thus from the law and replaced law with an inner spirit, He has granted to the Christian a liberty which religious obedience must not take away.

But St. Paul is careful to explain also that this freedom must not be used as a cloak for malice or to found a new servitude or slavery to sin. It is the task of obedience to develop this liberty, not to repress it. For the genuine slavery is the slavery to sin and to our own unguarded impulses. The law of the spirit has freed the Christian in Christ from the law of death and sin, restoring his genuine liberty, but in doing so, it has made the Christian a slave to justice and holiness, pointing out that his perfection is to be compared to the perfection of God Himself. Free from sin, the Christian makes himself a slave to God (Rom. 6: 13–18). However, this divine slavery is also a certain form of freedom, because to serve God is to reign.

Submitted to total charity, the religious and the Christian is delivered from lies, from errors; the truth has made him free. Since Christian obedience is always a freedom to do what is the will of God, superiors should provide for their subjects freedom to submit more fully to God in an ever-expanding liberty. The margin of discretion should be constantly enlarged for religious as they become more mature. We should be able legitimately to presume that they are arriving at the adult age of Christ, and that they will spontaneously follow the counsels of obedience without constant interruptions from without.

In the ancient form of religious life, the monastic form, obedience was of a special nature because of the special style of religious life. In the monastery, the abbot of the monastery represents the father of the family. He is, properly speaking, the father, and he is also the spiritual father to the subject. In this case, obedience has the special task of guiding those who live within a monastery towards sanctity and of preparing them in the spiritual life. Obedience also regulates the daily work of the monastery, but if the disciple has constantly to refer to the master it is for the purpose of learning from this spiritual father how to advance in holiness. The solicitude of the abbot for his children, the monks, remains always something paternal. The slightest details of life can be submitted to the will of the abbot.[11]

The great danger is, of course, that the monk will not develop to genuine adulthood. Therefore the abbot must exercise extraordinary prudence in fostering the development of the subject. Obedience is not supposed to render superfluous prudence, self-reflection, courage and greateartedness. Eventually, the monk must acquire initiative and decisiveness. The rule of St. Benedict insists upon the place which should be given to the advice of the brothers. According to the mind of St. Benedict, even the youngest monk may be called upon to give advice in the affairs of the monastery, and thus develop counsel, prudence and judgment. St. Thomas himself criticizes indiscreet obedience, disapproving of obedience which is without discernment, without judgment or prudence.

The superior must avoid any attempts to stifle the liberty, the judgment, or the critical spirit of his subjects. Instead, he should esteem himself happy to have the power to serve and to exercise his authority in the growth and development of his subject.

It is also the obligation of religious superiors to attempt to fulfill the natural aspirations and talents of their subjects. This duty is sometimes forgotten, and there has even been a belief, based on a false conception of mortification, that one must try to crush the natural talents of the subject for the sake of his spiritual progress. This is to forget that the minute laws and customs of the religious life are not, as we have constantly emphasized, absolute ends within themselves, but are means to assist in the formation of that style of life and that unity and charity which characterize religion. The superior's task is on the contrary, as we have said, to lead the subject to the full development of his personality in the particular style of the institute and to promote his interior liberty by freeing him from the remainders of childishness.

The religious soul who has renounced the world to seek God may legitimately expect that he will not truncate his personality or his spiritual development in obedience. He has a right to expect that he will grow as a man and as a Christian. Obedience is the virtue of a man, not that of a child or an animal. The best subjects are in fact not those who lack discernment or critical sense, conservatively clinging to tradition without analysis, and superiors will be in error if they regard as the most solid element in the community those who are devoid of initiative and opposed to all change. We have already noted Pius XII's strong insistence upon the need of making the subject of religious life complete in human development before we attempt to reform him spiritually.

If the exceptional student is a worry for educators today, we should ask ourselves also whether there is room in religious life for exceptionally gifted subjects, or whether the old adage "the good die young and the brilliant leave" should be accepted tranquilly. Religious life does not attempt to reduce all to the same level. The fate of the exceptional individual in the monastic life should not regularly be frustration.

In the apostolic orders and congregations which are more and more to the fore in the Church today religious life takes on a particular structure. Here the superior is less paternalistic and is usually elected for a limited period of time. Particular orders generally have very clearly determined objectives and are preoccupied in a large measure with definite activities. This type of order obviously demands initiative and responsibility on the part of its subjects. Obedience here organizes the life of the community and the activities of the ministry, but it should also educate the religious soul to initiative and attendance upon God. Very frequently in this active life there are profound demands made upon the religious, renouncements which reach his whole sphere of activity. Obedience can be very demanding in this form of life by touching all the minutiae of daily existence. Wherever possible the superior should confide more and more to the initiative of the subject, so that the subject may develop a loving docility to God and interior liberty in his apostolic life.

It is true that the religious learns to accept obedience as an education and a liberation. Not only is he formed to the innumerable rubrics of the religious life which bestow upon him a certain religious and humane elegance, but he is also taught to act not through pride or caprice or unreasonably but as a mature and self-possessed adult. When obedience constantly rectifies his conduct and directs his action he learns to consider objective law, the demands of charity and the common good. His zeal is then extended to further and further horizons. Selfish individualism is eliminated and the individual learns to obey boldly, to take the initiative courageously according to the spirit of his institute. By obeying he learns to become adult, gifted with judgment, prudence, critical sense and the ability to accept the decisions of others in his regard. He is freed from that slavery to sin, and the satisfactions of pride and the flesh, which are the danger of all Christians. Liberation from such slavery is doubtless painful. It is the royal road of the cross, but it is also a high imitation of Jesus Christ. The Christian life is a communion with the virtues of Christ, and He is the great obeyer. For He obeyed even unto death of the Cross. He learned by suffering what it was to obey, and the Christian follows this same road in the service of his Lord. Thus, obedience formally constitutes the religious, even more than do poverty and chastity, since it forms and directs his entire life.

The misconceptions concerning the nature of obedience make it difficult in religious life for many. Apart from the widespread errors concerning it, the fact is that it is not particularly easy from a theological point of view to justify the donation of one's personal liberty to God in order to obey a human superior. In the early Church sanctity was conceived primarily as a matter of martyrdom and secondarily as a matter of asceticism and of virginity. There is no record of religious obedience in early Christian times. Neither the Gospel nor St. Paul affirms the necessity or the desirability of such obedience. In view of these considerations, attention should be given to what the Church's attitude towards this form of life is.

The Church does not impose the religious form of life on anyone but leaves it up to the free choice of the individual. Moreover, it is not her intention that in the religious life the freedom which God has entrusted to us and which is our own inalienable responsibility should be surrendered absolutely to another. On the contrary, she very carefully watches over the constitution of religious orders, permitting superiors to command subjects only within the framework of the constitution which she herself, as the messenger of God, has approved as a way of holiness. It is not therefore, as we have already observed, the primary notion of obedience to surrender one's will to a human superior, but to surrender one's will to a definitely constituted form of life approved by the juridical and mystical Church.

The Church does not canonize for religious the kind of obedience that becomes a child. The obedience befitting childhood suggests that the child is lacking in personal maturity and that as soon as he has come to this maturity he will substitute his own free decisions for obedience to the parent. Hence, while religious obedience has an educative force, forming our liberty to sanctity, it does not imply that the one being educated is less intelligent, prudent, mature or gifted than the one who commands. Ascetical writers over the centuries have specifically pointed out that one should not obey because the religious superior is more holy, more prudent, more mature, or more efficient and discerning than is the subject. They do well to stress this, because such a motivation would destroy the supernatural character of obedience and would admit the possibility that obedience could no longer exist in certain situations.[12]

For the daily routine of community life religious obedience functions as a method which would doubtless be accepted by any rational man for the organization of a complex way of living. In many details of religious life, obedience is an orderly fashion of procedure determined by the constitutions or by the individual superiors. It would be very immature on the part of the subject to object to decisions of the superior in these small details. On the other hand, it would be equally immature of the superior to insist that all of these small details and all of the unimportant decisions he makes are under the direct sign of the Holy Spirit. Doubtless, too, the subject could provide a rational plan, but that is not the point. The mature subject dedicates his liberty to fulfilling the rational plan which has been decided upon by one juridically appointed to make the decision.

We have insisted upon the need for superiors to recognize their function of granting scope to the full employment of the natural and supernatural talents of their subjects. The religious should, therefore, be continuously guided throughout his religious life to further exploration of his own capabilities and initiatives. This initiative cannot be formed late in life; hence even young religious must be taught at once that the religious order is their concern and that they must interest themselves in its common work. The aim of religious obedience is in no way to render the subject a passive figure on a chessboard to be moved to and fro without criticism of the values embodied in the decision of the superior. On the contrary, the superior should count upon the initiative of the subject and invite it in an honest and straightforward way. Thus it is that without deceit and in mutual trust religious obedience and religious authority will flourish in grace under God.

NOTES

1. Mersch, *Morality and the Mystical Body*, p. 272.
2. F. Durrwell, "Sainteté Chrétienne, Sainteté d'Obéissance," in *Vie Spirituelle* (1956), p. 267.
3. F. Taymans, "Contrefaçons de l'Obéissance," in *Nouvelle Revue Théologique* (1945), p. 321.
4. *Ibid.*, p. 320.
5. T. Camelot, "Obéissance et Liberté," in *Vie Spirituelle* (1952), pp. 165–166.
6. K. Rahner, "A Basic Ignatian Concept: Some Reflections on Obedience," in *Woodstock Letters* (1957), p. 293.
7. A. Plé, "Obedience Leads to Maturity," in *Obedience* (Newman, Westminster, 1956), pp. 133–135.
8. Camelot, *art. cit.*, p. 167.
9. A. Motte, "The Theology of Religious Obedience," in *Obedience* (Newman, Westminster, 1956), pp. 66–67.
10. L. Beirnaert, "Enfance spirituelle et Infantilisme," in *Vie Spirituelle* (1951), pp. 379–380.
11. P. Régamey, "L'Épreuve de l'Obéissance," in *Vie Spirituelle* (1951), pp. 379–380.
12. Rahner, *art. cit.*, pp. 297–299.

Confidence in Prayer

7 Confidence in Prayer

There is probably no religious soul which, at some time or other in the course of its mature spiritual life, does not begin to wonder if it has drifted away from God. This can be a disturbing, even an agonizing, experience, the more so since the soul cannot point to any definite offence against its Lord. Its anguish results rather from the projection upon God of its own heavy sense of self-weariness and disgust. Feeling that God is at least as bored with it as it is with itself, it becomes discouraged at the shallowness of life, the pettiness of its choices, the endless battle against self. With a sense of dismay it feels itself at an infinite distance from God and His ways. In such a state of spiritual aridity, combined with the loss of the natural buoyancy of youth, there comes the depressing thought that the soul has squandered a multitude of graces, to the disappointment and displeasure of God. The result is a feeling of uneasiness, anxiety, and a profound sense of insecurity.

Psychologically, all men need the feeling of inner security. Too often, however, they try to obtain it through means which leave them even more deeply insecure. But the spiritually adult person knows that he can find his security only under God and within himself. It is only on the basis of an active faith in the all-powerful God who holds us in the hollow of His hand that man is able to recognize and reject the false securities of this life. In his desire to be understood and appreciated by others the Christian may not compulsively seek love and affection. Such a search for understanding and love would be really no search at all but only the yielding to an imperious inner demand to find temporary security in other human beings.

So too with the griefs with which human life is strewn, the necessary sorrow which comes to all men; misunderstandings, trials and failures normally cause us to experience even more profoundly our inner insecurity. Neither man nor God can preserve our interior unity in the face of infantile demands for love and protection. The Christian soul, strong in its faith that God commands every detail of its existence, knows that it cannot find security anywhere but in God, who leads it progressively to psychological maturity and the adult stature of Christ.

Only Christ, then, and His grace can create for us a milieu of security. The thought of His inexhaustible mercy should dispel any fear that His graces will be given less abundantly in the future because of our wretched use of them in the past. Theologically speaking, it is impossible to conceive of a limit to the mercy of God. At the primal source of all being is the love of the Father eternally donating His whole Nature to the Son. Self-donation is at the heart of reality itself. The realization that goodness has an immortal and infinite spring, that omnipotence is from eternity a source of self-donation and love, should be a powerful bulwark to our confidence.

To realize that God is infinitely merciful, infinitely faithful, we have only to recall the history of His dealings with man. From all eternity God had foreseen the sins of man; yet He created him and planned for him a Redeemer conspicuous for His mercy from beginning to end. All His life Christ consorted with sinners, but there is no record that they ever found Him hard, unyielding or wanting in comprehension. He chose the penitent Magdalen to be His apostle to the apostles on the morning of His resurrection. Moreover, those who fear that, having fallen from certain heights in the spiritual life, they will never again be given the same degree of holiness need only look at Peter, who was chosen for the closest friendship with Christ, betrayed that friendship, and was nevertheless restored to an even greater intimacy.

It is a want of confidence in the omnipotence of God to imagine that He mends us in a human fashion, poorly, so that all of the defects are visible still to His eyes. On the contrary, His triumphant power raises the sinner to new and more glorious life. His mercy stretches from eternity to eternity. It is not God who withdraws from man but man who withdraws from God, and even then He follows after. How often did He seek out the Jews with His prophets, with His angels, with His marvellous signs, and how often they withdrew from Him! He established a privileged race and a privileged family, and the whole history of Israel is one of God's rejection by man and His incredible ingenuity in seeking man out again.

This is also, of course, the history of the individual soul. "Even if a mother can forget the child of her womb," yet God cannot forget us (Is. 49:15). He compares Himself in Sacred Scripture to a woman in order that we may understand His tender love for the human soul. Surely He does this because He wishes us to trust in His creative mercy. God's love is not merely a love responsive to pre-existent values in us; it is a love creative of values in us. Throughout the life of Christ the motif of His actions was always "Come!"

The memory of past sins should not cause us to lacerate ourselves with reproaches. Such self-torture is usually motivated by pride. Rather should we content ourselves with the recognition that we are sinners and that such we shall always be, in comparison with the infinite purity of God. Moreover, we must realize that all we see is a partial picture, isolated defects. Many more faults would have to be recorded were our memory perfect and our examination one which plumbed the depths of our psychology. We would do well, then, to consider that it is our very wretchedness which attracts the mercy of God to raise us from our filth and to create us princes of His people. Truly, it is our very sickness which appeals to the Divine Physician. We must therefore hold to our confidence and hope against all hope.

God is good by essence; and since His very essence is identical with His goodness He rejoices in multiplying His benefits for the creatures He has drawn out of nothing for precisely this reason. Humanly speaking, God longs to make us happy, to communicate His goodness to us and so manifest His own glory. How can God resist the prayer of the

confident man for something which fulfills His will? It is
as though one appealed to an aspect of God's nature pe-
culiarly responsive to prayer. He has said that He will de-
liver us because we have known His name (Ps. 90:14). "Because he hoped in me, I will free him, I will protect him
because he has known my name." Here God gives as the
motive of His action not our goodness but the greatness of
His own divine essence. Even the sinner will be heard, because the sinner who prays confidently for redemption from
his sin has recognized the nature of the Redeemer. He has
offered to God a homage fitting to the nature of God. For
this reason, perhaps, St. Bernard affirms that confidence is
successful to the degree that it is daring in its hope.[1]

Doubtless the prayers of the man already possessing
sanctifying grace will be answered by a new burgeoning of
this state of sanctity, a new awakening of the forces of life
within him. For the presence of the Holy Spirit is a dynamism within the soul that seeks to expand its domain. In
such a soul the Holy Spirit is constantly laboring to cultivate
the new life of grace, to defend and conserve it. The confident prayer of such a man mingled with the groanings of
the Spirit infallibly brings down God's mercy.

Nor is God bound in the distribution of His grace by
impersonal laws which constrict His mercy. His graces are
not to be thought of in terms of impersonal, exteriorized,
physical forces but in terms of personal appeals. For God
knows how to activate all the forces of our human psychology to recall us to Him. Very frequently He uses periods
of silence, apparent absences, to awaken the soul to the
emptiness of its life. At other times He shakes it in thunder-
ing fashion, sharply prodding the conscience, injecting the
gall of bitterness and remorse. And He knows how to alter-

nate periods of drawing sweetness with those of stark strength. There are no elements of the human personality, even the most instinctual, into which God cannot insert His grace.[2]

He has, moreover, bound Himself in fidelity to reward the appeal of the sinner to His mercy. He has said to us: "Ask and you shall receive" (Mt. 7:28). He has said to us: "All that you ask of the Father in my name I will do" (John 14: 13–14); "When you ask for anything in prayer, you have only to believe that it is yours, and it will be granted you" (Mark 11: 22–24). Christ is not speaking for effect here, but is literally obliging Himself to grant us whatever we ask with the right dispositions. There is no deception, for it is not the function of the revealing Word of God, the Saviour of our intellects, to deceive us. And yet He places no limit whatsoever to our confidence, as though it were His intention to fulfill our longing for sanctity without reserve. Demanding a greathearted submission to His omnipotence, it is only that omnipotence which He sets as a limit to our confidence. "Ask in his name and you will receive."

It should be clear, however, that Christ has not bound Himself as to the manner in which He will answer our confident prayer. He who knows our future and our past, who knows what He Himself intends in the way of sanctity for us, uses His own procedures for bringing us to this goal. We have only to follow Him, even when appearances are not, so to speak, in the divine favor. Often His graces are concealed, entering so subtly into our lives that we fail to recognize them or even to distinguish them from natural forces. All the natural, external circumstances of our life are material for His hands, and He speaks to us in terms of incidents,

events, facts. There are hours when His graces are so calm
and apparently so uninterrupted, and in such continuity
with our ordinary life, that they seem to follow an almost
biological law of development. At other times there are
abrupt changes in the soul's spiritual climate, and God sets
in force subconscious natural drives that shake us to our
depths. Again, summoning up half-forgotten memories from
the dim background of our lives, He actuates them with His
divine inspiration. The very circumstances of the world
about us, our community, our friendships, our companions,
our tasks—all the events and facts of our lives—become
sacramentally charged by Him with new "mystery" and
new meaning.

Our confidence would be greatly increased if we had a
more thorough understanding of the nature of grace itself.
Sacred Scripture gives us the key by constantly accenting
the benevolence and mercy of God. The generous source of
all good, He lavishes upon man an interior gift which is inseparable from His love; for the love of God is efficacious.
When Sacred Scripture speaks of grace, it emphasizes
this subjective aspect rather than the objective gift conferred upon the beloved, although, of course, the two are
closely related. In the gift of grace that we receive from
God we must always behold the loving benevolence of the
Giver. To the soul in sanctifying grace God has given an
infinite gift of Himself to be really possessed. It should be
superfluous to insist that this possession of God by man
cannot come about as the result of any purely human asceticism, much less through any philosophical dialectic.
God gives His grace uniquely out of the depths of His own
liberty conferring itself upon the liberty of man. Grace

arises in man as the result of an absolutely gratuitous initiative upon the part of God. It is His intention to realize a union of wills between Himself and the human spirit. Once we have realized how absolutely gratuitous is God's grace and how closely connected with His infinite love, our confidence should become limitless.

The very word *grace* should inspire confidence in the heart of the Christian. In the ancient Greek literature from which this word was borrowed it implies something which shines, something which provokes joy in the beholder. So, too, the sanctifying grace with which God adorns the soul gives joy to His heart as grace and charm and lovability gladden the human heart. It is also notable that in ancient Greek literature grace refers directly to the benevolence, generosity and good favor of one who, without any compulsion, wishes to give joy and pleasure to another. This sentiment of one who is superior towards a beloved inferior, of the master towards his servants, is a disinterested goodness. We find this notion carried over in the Christian idea of grace. It is not, as we have said, our pre-existent merits which attract the mercy of God, it is His own liberality, generosity and benevolence which pour forth goodness upon us.

Again, in classical literature we have the word *grace* used for the generous gifts of the Emperor to his soldiers on his birthday. To the idea of benignity there is thus added the concept of the distribution of gifts. Who are we to say that one soldier was more worthy of these gifts than another? So, too, in the mystical and magical writings of the Hellenistic periods of Greek literature, we find that grace signifies a supernatural power poured into the soul by which man is capable of accomplishing prodigies. This same sense of power is carried over into Christian literature, and we see that the grace which God gives us in baptism is a dynamism, a power seeking development and deployment.

In the Greek translation of the Old Testament the word for grace implies the idea of physically leaning over someone. Thus, as a mother leans over her child in the crib, so God by His generous favor and benevolent love hovers over the soul upon whom He has conferred the gift of sanctifying grace. In the historical books of the Old Testament, *grace* constantly evokes the notion of the favor and the benevolence which the inferior finds in the eyes of Yahweh. We have found grace in the eyes of God (Gen. 6:8). The prophets of the Old Testament also imply this same idea of generosity when they speak of grace: "The people that were left and escaped from the sword, found grace in the desert . . ." (Jer. 31.2). In the last books of the Old Testament the notion of good, value, benefit is frequent when the word *grace* is used in its religious meaning. Grace, then, implies divine favor and perfectly free benignity and condescension on the part of Yahweh, the source of all benedictions.[3]

So it is that when we analyze the Old Testament use of the term *grace* we see that it constantly implies love on the part of the giver of benefits. Grace is an objective gift conferred upon the soul as a result of a subjective inner disposition on the part of God which is best described as love, benignity, kindness.

In the New Testament the word *grace* is certainly a Pauline favorite, and again the fundamental meaning in St. Paul is the gratuitous favor of God the Father, the liberal and merciful benevolence of God who pardons the sinner and overwhelms him with benefits. As it is God who has begun this great work of redemption in the human heart through the grace of baptism, so it is He who continues daily the work of bringing to its term the sanctity of the individual. In the words of St. Augustine, Christ constantly presses graces upon us: "Jesus demands that we ask; does He do this in order to refuse?"

When the Christian soul reflects upon the great gift of sanctifying grace which elevates him to a quasi-equality of nature with God, giving him a share in the divine nature as nature, as a principle of activity, he cannot but infer from this first manifestation of mercy and redemptive love that God will never desert the soul which He has invited to sanctity.

We must, moreover, strongly believe that God's redemptive intention regards us personally. We must be aware that He does not deal with us as nameless members of a congregation but focuses His gaze of infinite love on each of us individually. Incomprehensible though it may be to the human mind that the Infinite God should seek our love, nevertheless the Christian must realize that he is addressed by God and that God expects a return of love. Not even the clear memory of definite sins should separate us from our confidence in God, nor make us yield to the temptation to doubt His mercy. "God is faithful," though we are not.

It would, of course, be a great mistake to believe that we are truly confident in God when we rely upon the forces of our own nature, our talents, our efficiency, our natural gifts to provide for our future. Instead we are most powerful when we are weakest (2 Cor. 12:10). Our confidence must be a supernatural confidence, one that is based on a wholehearted commitment to the length and breadth of the Gospel message. Casting ourselves wholly free from the human security that natural gifts can bring us, we must direct the whole weight of our lives towards God. We must cling continually to the truths of our Faith, believing that God wills our redemption to the very depths of our souls, that there is no element in our lives which He does not will to redeem and to perfect.

We must not, however, look for experiential evidence that God is at work dictating every concrete detail of our life. There are moments, it is true, when the presence of God's love for us touches us with a sweet power and communicates itself almost sensibly, but these moments are rare. What we must do is to believe that the background of our entire existence is God's commitment to us, so that while our humility and contrition increase by our faults, our confidence increases to a corresponding degree. The faults which reveal our weakness reveal also the greatness of God's love, who intends to save us in spite of them.[4]

Generally speaking, it is not the great sins which cause loss of hope on the part of the sinner. The one who clearly recognizes great sins in his life often clearly recognizes his profound unhappiness without God and the deep orientation which he has towards God. By the very emptiness of a sinful life, he is often shaken to his depths and made to grasp his metaphysical situation more clearly. What tend to discourage most souls are rather the endless petty sins which seem to inhibit any progress in the spiritual life.

It is true that certain souls experience the apparent failure of grace within themselves and are seized with a sense of crisis in their trust of God. This is particularly true of those who seem to be afflicted with habitual deficiencies of a moral or psychological order. At times such souls appeal to the mystery of predestination, without realizing that this mystery in no sense implies any irrational preference of God for certain souls. The sovereign liberty of God has within it nothing of chance, absurdity or caprice. Although He does indeed have His friends, He sincerely, operatively wills the salvation of all men, and an immense and incalculable love presides over the mystery of His distribution of grace. Often, too, the apparent failures of His grace seem to be simply provisory—perhaps the prelude to and condition of an outpouring of an even greater mercy.

Doubtless, from our human point of view, there are times when His grace seems less victorious in certain sincere souls than we feel it ought to be. Yet this may simply be another indication of the sovereign mastery of God, who counts upon the whole of time to bring us to our destined holiness. When the Christian has honestly striven to overcome some habitual defect or vice, and finds himself apparently helpless in its grip, he should remember that God searches the depths of the human soul and that His mercy is infinite. This should be the background against which he projects all his defects. In God there is no shadow of alteration or change; this should be the unshaken ground upon which the Christian bases all possibility of growth for the future. His relationships with God should always be rooted in the truth that God, in the words of St. Augustine, is a seeing and living God. From this he will develop the confidence to go again and again to Christ in contrition, leaving it to Him to interpret the meaning of his particular flaws, trusting that He can turn even these to His glory and the sinner's merit.

It is true that there are things in life capable of frightening the most prudent person. The evil and hostility of men in power, the approach of death, illness, the loss of our natural certitudes and securities—all these tend to plunge the Christian into anguish. Yet all these menacing circumstances are only relative to God, and He has it within His power to alter them at will. As true Christians we should always contrast the transitory character of all these things with the enduring providence of God, and not fasten our gaze exclusively upon secondary causes as though the working out of these causes were inevitable and compelling. It is God who holds all secondary causes within the control of His knowledge and His will, and we should not be paralyzed with fear by the abyss they seem to open up before us. Whenever we are threatened with a genuine evil, we must realize that this evil is only partial and temporary, and that its avoidance is not an unconditioned good. Therefore we should pray: "Father, not my will, but Thy will be done," confident that our prayer will be heard by an infinitely wise and loving God.[5]

Sometimes authors speak of the supernatural order as if it were some sort of addition to the natural order, as if grace were an inert object resting in the depths of our souls. Actually, as we have seen, the great gift of grace is the product of an inner personal attitude on the part of God. The divine action which produces grace in us is similar to an act of loving affection on the part of a human friend. Grace is not a thing, not an impersonal block or force; it is primarily a relationship between persons. Like all such relationships it tends to create an erosphere, a "we" of two persons. We can thus speak to God as to one who has no need to act as an extrinsic force or as a psychological pressure, but can move us gently yet forcibly by provoking our own liberty into action. It is thus that He disposes the will ahead of time to accept the gift which He intends to give us. For though our sanctity comes primarily as a gift from Him, yet it is not given without our consent. The mystery is that even the consent itself is given by Him and may be called a grace.

When we pray for a given good which we feel will benefit us, we should pray with confidence, but we should also realize that it is God's intention above all that we pray for the supremely great good of eternal salvation. All other goods are lesser goods, subservient to this good, and God alone, who knows our future and our destiny, is best able to judge whether a certain good suits us at this particular historical stage of our development. Hence we should never feel that God has not answered our prayers. His love is not partial and deficient; it is total and infinitely knowledgeable, whereas our vision of creation and the circumstances of our life is imperfect and finite. We should not, therefore, think of prayer as something mechanical or magical. Prayer is simply a natural reaction to the situation of personal dialogue in which God has placed us and, as such, it is never unheard.

The sincere person who, after many years, still finds within himself what seem to be the same defects he experienced at the beginning of his spiritual life should not lose hope but rather rejoice, knowing that if he is still in the state of sanctifying grace, God has already brought about the essential cure of his nature. From being ill, weakened, and inclined to sin he has become sanctified. This is why the Christian should take courage: whatever the power of instinctual forces within him, whatever the threats of evil without, and whatever the defects of his conduct, his deepest value is still that he is one whom God loves.

It is true also that external observation and even inner psychological reflection cannot give us a perfect understanding of our whole moral value. We must be patient with ourselves, for there may be elements in our lives which do not engage our entire responsibility. Provided one is in the state of sanctifying grace, there is no longer a fundamental obstacle to the mutual relation of love which God has established between Himself and the soul. Again, we are not in a position to register psychologically the graces which God is giving us at the present moment. He works mysteriously, in depths unavailable to psychological reflection. As we have seen, the body itself, the visible temple of the Holy Spirit, is responsive even in its instinctual life to the touch of the Spirit, and it is He who joins His prayers to man's for his purification.

God is able to work in the very depths of the psychological life, what the mystics call the fine point of the spirit; He can also penetrate the body of man to prepare it organically to respond to grace. As we have said again and again in this chapter, there is no area of human life, even the most instinctual, which grace does not penetrate. It is the grace of Christ and, as incarnate, completely adapted to our human nature. It is able to sound all the depths of our conscience, intellect, memory and will, to touch our affectivity as well as persuade our intelligence; the assistance of our organic faculties is open to its workings. On certain temperaments its influence is calming; others are stirred into activity by brusque invitations and interior demands; intractable wills are bent to the purpose of sanctity. It is able to present itself under every form of our imaginative life. In the same vital fashion in which the human body is able to wall up foreign obstacles introduced into itself, grace can seal off obstacles to its own operation. It is able to speak in season and out of season.[6]

At times the Christian sees what appears to be the triumph of evil. This is, of course, an impenetrable mystery. Yet our belief in God and our confidence in Him must remain unshaken. We must not imagine that God has become indifferent to us because for the moment He allows the powers of darkness to have their way. On the contrary, we must believe that the evil which God permits has its own mysterious meaning and purpose, which God does not intend to reveal. For us this is a test. We must face it, and refusing to be bewildered by the evil in this life, we must calmly pursue our struggle for the good, though the result may seem to be failure, even to the point of martyrdom. What God calls for in the face of the triumph of evil is neither fatalistic resignation nor quietistic inactivity, but simply a tranquil confidence that in the end He will triumph and that He will draw some good from the momentary progress of evil. We must never forget that all reality is in the power of the Reality of the living God, who has a face and a voice.

There will even be in the lives of most Christians moments of spiritual darkness in which they are tempted to wonder if God has not forsaken them. In such periods the heart seems to be completely without affection, prayer is arid, inspiration disappears and all human enterprises turn to failure. The soul becomes aware only of its own spiritual deficiencies and powerlessness. This too is a word from God. Therefore, we must not lose hold of our conviction that He has an unchanged awareness of our needs. We must not allow the truth to be obscured that God is a loving God who has addressed us by name, and that He does not repent of His choice of us. Often His grace is at work within us at that depth where we take our definitive options, knowing our full responsibility. Christ resides here, and His spirit completes the prayer of man, so that even in this dark night of the soul there will still at times be fugitive intimations of the presence of God. It is the part of faith to accept the fact that God is active within us.

Sometimes the Christian will feel certain that this supernatural darkness is the result of his own defects and sins, but he should remember that even were this true, actual grace acts in the sinner as an anticipation of the divine life which is to come, soliciting his conscience by new demands and modulating his prayer. Even in the sinner grace inspires decisions that illumine the intelligence and transform the psychological life. The visible exercise of the virtues in the moral order is simply a projection to the exterior sphere (the visibility of grace, as it were) of that friendship which unites the soul and its God. When the period of darkness is past, the mystic takes a fuller awareness of God's love and is thereafter more and more completely drawn to perfect acquiescence to the divine activity.

Grace is the fulfillment of a divine initiative, commanded entirely by love in all its perspectives. The gift which God intends to make to the soul in grace is the gift of His own personality which transcends all earthly goods, all earthly vocations, and all human desires. From the moment in which man rejects voluntary sin, the redemptive decision has been posed, and God cannot but treat the conscience of the sinner after the fashion of His own plenitude.

Our hopes are in the Lord, knowing our own weakness but trusting in His power. Let us, then, despite the anguish of our sensibility and the inquietude of our imagination, walk in naked faith to Him who defines Himself as Charity, asking all things for His glory, in His name, confident that He will accomplish them in order that the Father may be glorified also in us.

NOTES

1. Dietrich von Hildebrand, *Transformation in Christ* (New York, Longmans, 1948), pp. 159–160.
2. E. Rideau, "La Grace du Christ," in *Nouvelle Revue Théologique* (1947), pp. 898–899.
3. J. Guillet, *Thèmes Biblique* (Paris, Aubier, 1951), pp. 26–29.
4. H. Rondet, "La Grace Libératrice," in *Nouvelle Revue Théologique* (1947), p. 129.
5. von Hildebrand, *op. cit.*, pp. 159–160.
6. Rideau, *art. cit.*, p. 903.